# THE GOD OF JESUS CHRIST

JOSEPH CARDINAL RATZINGER
(Pope Benedict XVI)

# The God of Jesus Christ

## Meditations on the Triune God

*Translated by Brian McNeil*

Second Edition

With a Foreword by Leonard J. DeLorenzo

IGNATIUS PRESS    SAN FRANCISCO

Original German edition:
*Der Gott Jesu Christi: Betrachtungen über den Dreieinigen Gott*
© 1976 by Kösel-Verlag, Munich
New edition: 2006

Cover art: *The Baptism of Christ*
by Fra Angelico
Museo di San Marco, Florence, Italy
© Scala / Art Resource, New York

Cover design by Roxanne Mei Lum

DEDICATED

TO MY BROTHER PRIESTS
ON THE OCCASION OF THE SILVER JUBILEE
OF OUR ORDINATION

1951–1976

# CONTENTS

# FOREWORD TO THE
# SECOND EDITION

In his book *The Trinity*, Karl Rahner memorably remarked that, "despite their orthodox confession of the Trinity, Christians are, in their practical life, almost mere 'monotheists.' We must be willing to admit that, should the doctrine of the Trinity have to be dropped as false, the major part of religious literature could well remain virtually unchanged."[1] Rahner detected a poverty of the Christian imagination, one where imprecision and flatness in the presentation of the faith finds its match in the diminished quality of the "lived faith" of believers. Taking his two lines together and inserting them into the mold of a cherished Patristic maxim, we might summarize his words by saying, *Whatever is not preached is not believed.*

Joseph Ratzinger preaches the beauty of the Trinity. Though emerging from great theological learning and deep knowledge of the Church's faith, his preaching is conducted in the manner of all good preaching: with concern for the "practical life" of Christians as well as would-be Christians. With both understanding and compassion, he preached Lenten sermons in the church of Saint Emmeram in Regensburg; he preached Advent sermons in Freiburg; he preached a sermon on the jubilee of the Council of Nicaea, again in Regensburg; he preached an Easter address

[1] Karl Rahner, *The Trinity*, trans. Joseph Donceel (New York: Crossroad, 1997), 10–11.

9

over the airwaves of Bavarian Radio; and he preached retreats in seminaries and monasteries, all the time standing on the rock of the Church's faith while speaking to the hearts and minds of men and women who have their own questions, uncertainties, difficulties, joys, and devotions. He preached, and, as he preached, he strove to "build a bridge between theology and spirituality, thereby aiding the [listeners] to assimilate personally what the Church's faith seeks to express" (21). When these various sermons were drawn together into one collection, those "listeners" became "readers" who encountered this book: *The God of Jesus Christ*.

The effect of these sermons is to show that what Karl Rahner rightly observed is not a permanently settled fact. Ratzinger shows that the practical life of Christians always already bears the marks of the triune God so that the rediscovery of the beauty of who "God is" will be, at the same time, the rediscovery of the beauty of the Christian life. The key to renewing the Christian imagination is proclaiming *the mystery of God* in full volume, with all its splendid colors, in a way that is at once inviting and inspiring. Ratzinger preaches theology—the *logic of God*—so as to aid in the revival of the Christian imagination that animates the life of the believer and the practice of the Church.

The challenge for the preacher, of course, concerns not only the content with which he hopes to fill his sermon but also the disposition of the listener—or reader—who will receive this preached word. With modern audiences in disparate settings who might each, in one way or another, suffer from disinterest in lofty matters or things too heady and too far removed from the "stuff of life", the challenge to preaching *the mystery of God* is great indeed. In the face of this great challenge, the simple genius of Ratzinger's approach becomes apparent.

At the beginning of his sermon "'... and became man'", what Ratzinger says about his intention for that particular occasion is the key to his preaching of the Church's dogma from beginning to end: "All I wish to do is to look for a little theological lane, so that we can learn to grasp that which is great and far away on the basis of that which is near at hand and simple, something that touches our own lives" (79). He wishes to begin with the things that are familiar to us, the things that we see as concerning our "practical life", and then from there move little by little toward that which we do not yet understand but may grow to understand with the right kind of guidance. From the images and concerns that we already know, he will try to lead us along "a little theological lane" to discover something true about who "God is". What we will discover along the way is that we are also learning to see our starting point in a wholly new light because of what we find in God—that is, we rediscover ourselves as the ones God creates, redeems, and loves within that dialogical space between the Father and the Son that is the Holy Spirit.

Throughout this accessible text, Ratzinger proves the truth of what the *Catechism of the Catholic Church* states about the relationship between the central mysteries of the faith and the spiritual life lived in the Church: "There is an organic connection between our spiritual life and the dogmas. Dogmas are lights along the path of faith; they illuminate it and make it secure. Conversely, if our life is upright, our intellect and heart will be open to welcome the light shed by the dogmas of faith" (no. 89). Dogma preached well transforms those who receive this preaching, and those who have opened themselves to the light of faith find themselves ready to receive more of the mystery of God. The grammar of Christian belief is not the stuff

of faith itself (strictly speaking), and yet this grammar—
the ways of speaking of God—provides reliable pointers
to who "God is", allowing those practicing the Christian
faith to speak together in common and with understanding, while also safeguarding Christians from projecting
their own private images of God through their own pre-
ferred ways of speaking. The formulas of the faith respond
to who God has revealed himself to be—as Father, Son,
and Holy Spirit—and teach the Church and her faithful how both to welcome and to seek their beginning
and their end. Ratzinger knows well the importance of
this grammar, and his sermons do more than emphasize
its importance—they actually reveal its poetic order in
motion. In short, he aids his listeners and readers in learning how to speak of God from within their "practical life".
These lessons in the language of faith—captured in longer
form in his classic text *Introduction to Christianity* and more
fully developed in the longer work that stands behind this
present one, *Dogma and Preaching*—make apparent another
statement from the *Catechism*:

> We do not believe in formulas, but in those realities they
> express, which faith allows us to touch. "The believer's act
> [of faith] does not terminate in the propositions, but in the
> realities [which they express]" (Thomas Aquinas, *STh* II-
> II, 1, 2, *ad* 2). All the same, we do approach these realities
> with the help of formulations of the faith which permit
> us to express the faith and to hand it on, to celebrate it in
> community, to assimilate and live on it more and more.
> (no. 170)

Ratzinger seeks to transfer faith in the triune nature of
God from the realm of theoretical proposition to a spiritual knowledge that addresses men and women in their

"practical life". In itself, this is something of an incarnational move: the mysteries of the faith seek to take flesh in the embodied belief, discipleship, prayer, and hope of the Christian, within the liturgical and prophetic life of the Church. By slowly reading the lines of these sermons, one is likely to experience a whole web of meaning opening up. The connections that become apparent among these sermons often reach toward Ratzinger's other works where he develops many of these "preached" meditations in more detail. All the same and in each case, the inquirer is primarily thrown back, not to the integral nature of Ratzinger's own thought, but indeed to the intricate interweaving of all the mysteries of the faith. It is the wholeness of the Christian faith that orders Ratzinger's meditations, and it is the wholeness of God— One, in Persons three—who gives order to the Church's faith. Here as much as anywhere else, Ratzinger proves himself to be the consummate catechetical theologian, the ecclesial scholar, the preaching educator, who, in doing his work, grants access to a vast treasury: the life of faith held within the life of God.

The manner of Ratzinger's preaching provides an insight into his vocation as teacher of the faith, which is a vocation he admired in those who came before him and who educated him both in the content and the communication of the faith. Saint Augustine would certainly stand at the top of that list for Ratzinger, but even his immediate predecessors in the service of the teaching office of the Church provided him with an efficacious witness. In Ratzinger's 1988 foreword commemorating the forty-year anniversary of Henri de Lubac's *Catholicism*, what he says of his older contemporary is illuminative of the kind of service to the Church and her faithful that Ratzinger himself sought to imitate:

What is most engaging, however, is that de Lubac is not expressing his own private opinions, which would fade as they had blossomed, but lets the Fathers of our Faith speak so that we hear the voice of the origin in all its freshness and astonishing relevance. Whoever reads de Lubac's book will see how much more relevant theology is the more it returns to its center and draws from its deepest resources. This book is not clinging to a dead past. De Lubac is in dialogue with what is said by our most modern contemporaries. He hears it not as an outsider, but as one who is deeply sympathetic. Their questions are his own. He reads the Bible and the Fathers with the problems that we wrestle with in mind, and because he asks real questions, he finds real answers—and the Fathers become our contemporaries.[2]

Throughout de Lubac's text—as Ratzinger read it and we may read it alongside him—it is clear that de Lubac is accomplishing a tremendous amount of theological work, and yet his voice does not stand out as singular, such as one who seeks to draw praise from others. Rather, de Lubac gives his voice over to the common voice of the Church, taking on the role of one who listens and who bridges. He listens to the Fathers of the faith and, through them and with them, to the Bible, while also listening to the concerns and questions of his own contemporaries, both "within" and "outside" the Church. De Lubac's role is to build bridges between all those whom he hears through the words that he himself speaks and writes. In this way, his personal vocation is an ecclesial vocation, which is precisely what Ratzinger admires and seeks to embody in his own preaching and teaching.

[2] Henri de Lubac, *Catholicism: Christ and the Common Destiny of Man*, trans. Lancelot Sheppard and Elizabeth Englund (San Francisco: Ignatius Press, 1988), 11.

This brings us back to that method which Ratzinger employs throughout these sermons: always to begin with "something that touches our own lives" and, from there, move toward those things that seem "great and far away". If he learned from de Lubac how to give his voice over to the voice of the Church while doing theology, it was from Romano Guardini that he learned how to "preach theology" to his own contemporaries in such a way that the fruits of his efforts would be both growth in listeners' understanding and nourishment of their own spiritual life. It is well known that Guardini's liturgical theology shaped Ratzinger and led the latter to give his own text the same title as his teacher's—*Spirit of the Liturgy*—and yet Guardini's inspiration expands far beyond this most obvious occasion, becoming evident throughout Ratzinger's opus in myriad ways. For example, even in a lesser known text by Guardini—*Learning the Virtues that Lead You to God*—we discover the model for Ratzinger's method in these sermons: "To see all this is important for our understanding of the moral life of different individuals. It is also important for our own daily life, because in our moral development, it is well to begin with that which is familiar to us and then to advance to the conquest of that which is more alien."[3] Guardini was intellectually steeped in unparalleled theological and cultural depth, but he reaches out to his readers with sweetness, lightness, and familiarity, and in a sort of vernacular of common interests to allow that which is "more alien" actually to mean something. All the vast learning that Guardini had achieved remains hidden underground, as a foundation, rather than flaunted and advertised to draw esteem from awestruck onlookers, like pyrotechnics

[3] Romano Guardini, *Learning the Virtues that Lead You to God* (Manchester, N.H.: Sophia Institute Press, 1998), 12.

at a rock concert. This is as true of a text like *Learning the Virtues that Lead You to God* as it is of a far more massive text like his classic *The Lord*, for which Ratzinger himself wrote an introduction.[4]

Far from an innovative method that just happens to find success in communicating the mysteries of the faith, this manner of preaching and teaching that Ratzinger discovered in Guardini and others properly grows from and is inherently conducive to the salvific work of God, which is to say, it is founded on God's own manner of speaking. The humility and creativity of the teacher of the faith is conformed to the humility and creativity of the Word himself. Indeed, it is not only *what* is spoken about in these sermons that is of great importance, but also the *way* of speaking, which presents something of the saving mysteries. To grasp this point, it is helpful to turn to the latter pages of Ratzinger's second volume of *Jesus of Nazareth*, where he pens some of his more mellifluous words—words that praise the beauty of God's own "preaching":

> It is part of the mystery of God that he acts so gently, that he only gradually builds up *his* history within the great history of mankind; that he becomes man and so can be overlooked by his contemporaries and by the decisive forces within history; that he suffers and dies and that, having risen again, he chooses to come to mankind only

[4] See Romano Guardini, *The Lord*, trans. Elinor Castendyk Briefs (Washington, D.C.: Regnery Publishing Company, 2013), xi–xiv. In this manner of preaching and teaching, Ratzinger, like Guardini before him, seems to be healing the unfortunate divide between theology and spirituality that Hans Urs von Balthasar decried in his essay on "Theology and Sanctity" (see Hans Urs von Balthasar, *Explorations in Theology*, vol. 1: *The Word Made Flesh*, trans. A. V. Littledale and Alexander Dru [San Francisco: Ignatius Press, 1989], 181–209).

through the faith of the disciples to whom he reveals himself; that he continues to knock gently at the doors of our hearts and slowly opens our eyes if we open our doors to him.

And yet—is not this the truly divine way? Not to overwhelm with external power, but to give freedom, to offer and elicit love. And if we really think about it, is it not what seems so small that is truly great? Does not a ray of light issue from Jesus, growing brighter across the centuries, that could not come from any mere man and through which the light of God truly shines into the world? Could the apostolic preaching have found faith and built up a worldwide community unless the power of truth had been at work within it?[5]

In the final analysis, it is in fact the *Word of God* that begins with what is close and familiar, who draws near to listen, who takes on our language, who starts with our concerns, and from there leads those whose cares he takes on back up toward that one great thing which seems so very far away: life in God. The Word of God does not wait for those he seeks to understand him before coming to them, but rather opens a way to understanding by working for them and, by the Spirit he sends, in them. Even if "the doctrine of the Trinity" were dropped as false, the work of the Trinity would continue to heal, redeem, and sanctify, and, in the fullness of time, the understanding of what *has been done* would lead to unending praise. Through his own sermons, Ratzinger seeks to teach those who are still on their way to knowing God, and therefore truly knowing themselves, by beginning, over and over again, with that with which we

[5] Pope Benedict XVI, *Jesus of Nazareth, Part II: Holy Week: From the Entrance into Jerusalem to the Resurrection* (San Francisco: Ignatius Press, 2011), 276–77.

are familiar in order to help us see the beauty of the love that supports and surrounds us, making us more welcoming of this love through the renewal of our minds (see Rom 12:2).

Leonard J. DeLorenzo, Ph.D.
McGrath Institute for Church Life
University of Notre Dame
November 1, 2017
Solemnity of All Saints

# FOREWORD TO THE
## 2006 GERMAN EDITION

These meditations on the triune God and on the Incarnation of God in Christ provide a bridge between theology and proclamation, between theology and piety, which today more than ever have reference to each other and yet time and again stand in danger of drifting apart.

The first meditations seek to transfer faith in the triune nature of God from a theoretical proposition to a spiritual knowledge that addresses man in his personal life. The second group of meditations explores the passage "He came down from heaven" and develops the statement "He became man" on the basis of the concrete content of Jesus' humanity. A meditation on the Resurrection of the Lord rounds out the christological part. A final meditation addresses the theme of the Holy Spirit and considers it in comparison with the new experiences of the Spirit in the charismatic movement and with the hopes of the philosophy of history.

# PREFACE

In the spring of 1973, I was invited to preach the Lenten sermons in the church of Saint Emmeram in Regensburg, and this gave me the opportunity to try out in practice some of the principles that I had recently elaborated in my book *Dogma und Verkündigung* (Munich, 1973). The first and third chapters of the present volume are a revised version of those sermons; they are based on the theses that I had sketched in that book under the title "Preaching about God Today". The second chapter is based on Advent meditations that I held in Freiburg in December 1972; I have also included the sermon I preached at the celebration of the jubilee of the Council of Nicaea in Regensburg in 1975 and an Easter address that I gave on Bavarian Radio. I have drawn in various forms on this material in retreats I have given in Bad Imnau, in the seminary in Cologne, and in the abbey of Maria Laach. In the course of preparing these retreats, the texts, which had been written on various occasions, came together to form the unity in which they are presented here.

I hope that despite their various inadequacies—which are due to the diverse circumstances in which they were composed—these meditations may help build a bridge between theology and spirituality, thereby aiding the reader to assimilate personally what the Church's faith seeks to express.

Pentling, on the feast of Saints Peter and Paul, 1976

Joseph Ratzinger

I

# God

# God has names

We can all still remember how Yuri Gagarin returned from his space flight—the first in the history of mankind—and remarked that he had not seen a God anywhere. Now, even at that time it was obvious to a reflective atheist that this was not exactly a compelling argument against the existence of God. For even without Gagarin, we know that God cannot be touched with our hands or seen through telescopes; he does not live on the Moon, on Saturn, or on any other planet or fixed star. And it is not irrelevant to note that this space flight, although it represented a tremendous achievement on the part of man, scarcely amounted to more than a few steps out of one's own front door when measured against the vastness of the universe. Indeed, Gagarin himself saw far less than scientists already knew about the universe thanks to their calculations and observations.

The oppressive sense of the absence of God, which has left its mark on us all today, found much more profound expression many centuries ago in a Jewish fable that relates that the prophet Jeremiah and his son one day succeeded in creating a living man through the correct combination of words and letters. On the forehead of the Golem—the man whom they themselves had formed—were the letters that had helped to solve the riddle of creation: "Yahweh is the truth." The Golem tore off one of the seven letters that add up to this affirmation in Hebrew, and now the inscription proclaimed: "God is dead." The prophet and his son were horrified and asked the Golem what he was doing. The new man replied as follows: Now that you are able to create a man, God is dead.[1] My life is the death of God. Where man has all the power, God has no longer any power.

This ancient Jewish story, conceived in the Christian Middle Ages, is like a dream in which our fears are articulated: and it reveals the distress of man in today's technological age. Man possesses total power over the world. He analyzes its functions completely and is acquainted with the laws that govern its functioning. His knowledge is power. He can, so to speak, dissect the world and put it back together again; he regards the world as a functioning system that he uses and that he compels to serve him. In a world that is completely analyzed in this way, there is no longer any place for an intervention by God. Man

[1] Cf. W. Kern, "Tod Gottes und technisches Zeitalter: Umfeld und Vorgeschichte des humanistischen Atheismus", *Stimmen der Zeit* 190 (1972): 219–29, with historical background information and a detailed account of the story, which goes back to a pseudepigraphical text written in Languedoc at the beginning of the thirteenth century and is ascribed to the Mishnaic teacher Juda ben Bathyra. Kern shows that the atheistic point that we find here is unique in the mediaeval Golem tradition—in other texts, man's ability to reproduce the work of creation is presented as a demonstration of the greatness of God. Cf. also G. Scholem, *Zur Kabbala und ihrer Symbolik* (Zurich, 1960), pp. 234f. and 209–59; H. Thielicke, *Der evangelische Glaube* I (Tübingen, 1968), pp. 328–31. I believe that we find another striking example of the emergence of the atheistic question in the very heart of religious traditions in the prayer book of Duchess Dorothea of Prussia (1531), in which verses 6–7 of Psalm 6 ("I am weary with my moaning; every night I flood my bed with tears; I drench my couch with my weeping. My eye wastes away because of grief, it grows weak because of all my foes") appear in the following version: "I actually wished that you might not exist, rather than that I should continue to be tormented by you." Here, the suffering inflicted by God becomes a reason to wish that God might not exist. (Text in I. Gundermann, *Untersuchungen zum Gebetbüchlein der Herzogin Dorothea von Preussen* [Cologne and Opladen, 1966], plate II = folio 39v of the prayer book).

can find help only in man, since it is only man who has power over the world. But since a God without power is no God, there is no longer any God where man alone possesses power. These considerations also show us one fundamental aspect of the question of man's knowledge of God. We see that, ultimately, the knowledge of God is not a purely theoretical matter: it depends on the relationship that a man establishes between himself and the world and between his own self and his life. The problem of power is only one aspect; on a deeper level, this depends on prior decisions taken in the relationship to one's own "I", to "you", and to "us"—in the experience of being loved or being rejected. The fundamental experiences and decisions in this interplay between "I", "you", and "we" determine how a man sees the presence with him, and antecedent to him, of the One who is utterly other: Is he a competitor, a danger, or a reason for confidence? And this in turn determines whether man in the long run is compelled to contradict this Witness or to say Yes to him in reverence and thankfulness.

This reflection leads us to the real starting point of the question of God, which is much more basic than the dispute about proofs of God's existence, and I would therefore like to make it a little clearer with the help of the history of religions. In the religious history of mankind, which is completely identical with our intellectual history even in the birth of the high cultures, God is represented everywhere as the being with eyes on all sides, as the act of absolute seeing.[2] This archaic idea is preserved in the image

---

[2] For extensive material on this subject from the history of religions, cf. R. Pettazzoni, *Der allwissende Gott* (Frankfurt, 1957). On the problems involved, cf. E. Biser, "Atheismus und Theologie", in *Die Frage nach Gott*, ed. J. Ratzinger, pp. 89–115 (Freiburg, 1972).

of God's eye, with which we are familiar in Christian art:
God is an eye; God is the act of seeing. And behind this
lies a fundamental experience of man: he knows that he is
known. He knows that there is no definitive hiddenness.
He knows that his life lies open at every point to an act of
seeing, from which there is no concealment or escape. His
life is a state of "being seen". One of the most beautiful
psalms in the Old Testament is a prayer that expresses a
conviction that has accompanied man throughout all his
history (Ps 139 [138]:1–12):

> O Lord, you have searched me and known me!
> You know when I sit down and when I rise up;
>     you discern my thoughts from afar.
> You search out my path and my lying down,
>     and are acquainted with all my ways.
> Even before a word is on my tongue,
>     behold, O Lord, you know it altogether.
> You beset me behind and before,
>     and lay your hand upon me....
> Where shall I go from your Spirit?
>     Or where shall I flee from your presence?
> If I ascend to heaven, you are there!
>     If I make my bed in Sheol, you are there!
> If I take the wings of the morning
>     and dwell in the uttermost parts of the sea,
> even there your hand shall lead me,
>     and your right hand shall hold me.
> If I say, "Let only darkness cover me,
>     and the light about me be night,"
> even darkness is not dark to you,
>     the night is as bright as the day;
>     for darkness is as light with you.

As I have said, man can understand this state of "being seen" in directly antithetical ways. He can see it as an exposure that disturbs him. He can sense a danger therein and feel that the sphere of his life is restricted—a feeling that can turn to bitterness, leading to a passionate struggle against the Witness who is felt to be envious of man's own freedom and of the unlimited nature of man's desires and activities. However, the opposite can also happen. In this presence that surrounds him everywhere, man—who is created for love—can find the security for which his whole being cries out. He can see this as the overcoming of that loneliness which no man can abolish, although it is the utter contradiction of a being who yearns so deeply for a "you", for a life that is shared. In this hidden presence, man can find a reason for confidence, something that allows him to live. It is here that the question of God is decided. It depends on how a man considers his life on the deepest level. Does he want to remain unseen? Does he want only to be alone—"You will be like God!"? Or, despite and indeed because of his inadequacies, is he grateful for the One who is deeper than all his solitudes and supports these? The outcome here depends, once again, on many factors. It goes back to experiences with the "you" that leave their mark on a man: Does the "you" appear as love or as a menace? It also depends on the form in which God first meets a man—as the terrifying police guard who is inexorably bent on punishing us or as the creative love that is waiting for us. And it depends on those decisions in the course of a man's life in which he personally affirms or transforms his early experiences.

These reflections have made one thing clear: namely, that it is impossible to separate the question of whether God exists from the question of who or what God is. It is completely impossible to begin by proving or disproving the existence of God and then to begin pondering who or what God actually is. The contents that an image of God holds for a man are a fundamentally decisive factor in determining whether or not knowledge can develop here. And this knowledge and these contents are so profoundly interwoven with the basic decisions of human life, which limit or open up the sphere of a man's knowledge, that mere theory is impotent here.

Let us now ask: What does the God of the Bible look like? Who is he in fact? In the history of the biblical revelation in the Old and New Testaments, God's presentation of himself to Moses, as related in Exodus 3, proves again and again to be fundamental, on ever-deepening levels. It is important to begin by noting the historical and geographical framework of this narrative. The historical framework can be seen in God's words: "I have seen the affliction of my people who are in Egypt, and have heard their cry because of their taskmasters. I know their sufferings" (3:7). God is the protector of his people's rights. He protects the right of the powerless against the mighty. This is his true face, and this is the core of the Old Testament legislation that repeatedly extends God's personal protection to the widow, the orphan, and the stranger. This is the heart of Jesus' preaching, too. He himself took on the defenselessness of one who was accused and condemned and died, thereby extending the protection of God to this defenselessness. His struggle to clarify the meaning of the sabbath belongs in this context (like so much else in his life). In the Old Testament, the sabbath is the day when creatures have freedom, the day on which man and beast, slave and master, rest. It is the day on which the fraternal fellowship of all the creatures is reestablished in the midst of a world where equality and freedom are absent. On the sabbath, the creation returns for a moment to its point of origin. On the sabbath, all are free, thanks to God's own freedom. Jesus' working on the sabbath is not directed against the sabbath. Rather, he is fighting to establish its original meaning, preserving it as the day of God's freedom, so that the hands of the casuists may not pervert it into the opposite, that is, a day of tormented petty-mindedness.[3]

The event of Exodus 3 takes place in the wilderness, which is the place of vocation and of preparation for Moses, for Elijah, and for Jesus. There is no experience of God unless one goes out from the business of everyday living and accepts the confrontation with the power of solitude. From the first perspective, the historical framework, we must conclude that a heart consumed by desires, a self-seeking heart, cannot know God. From this second perspective, we can affirm that a heart in which there is a din, a heart that is inattentive, a heart that is not recollected, cannot find God.

Let us come to the heart of the matter. God gives himself a name when he speaks to Moses and expounds this name in the formula: "I am who I am."[4] The event is inexhaustible: everything that will follow in the history of faith, up to and including Jesus' own confession of God, is an ever-renewed exposition of these words, which thereby acquire an ever-greater depth. At a very early date, it is clear that this explanation marks off the name "Yahweh" from the

---

[3] Cf. T. Maertens, *Heidnisch-jüdische Wurzeln der christlichen Feste* (Mainz, 1965), pp. 114–47.

[4] On this exposition, cf. especially R. P. Merendino, *Der unverfügbare Gott: Biblische Erwägungen zur Gottesfrage* (Düsseldorf, 1969); T. Schneider, *Plädoyer für eine wirkliche Kirche* (Stuttgart, 1972), pp. 24–31; A. Deissler, *Die Grundbotschaft des Alten Testaments*, 2nd ed. (Freiburg, 1972); J. Ratzinger, *Einführung in das Christentum*, 10th ed. (Munich, 1970), pp. 84–102. The comparison between name and number was suggested to me by my student C. del Zotto.

divine names that exist everywhere in the world. This is not one name among many, because the One who bears this name is not one among many gods who share the same being. His name is a mystery. His name makes him utterly incomparable. "I am who I am"—this means closeness, power over the present and over the future. God is not the prisoner of what happened "before all eternity"; he is always presence: "I *am*." He is contemporary with every time and antecedent to every time. I can call on this God here and now: he belongs to the "now" and responds to my "now".

Centuries later, at the end of the great exile, another aspect becomes decisive. The powers of the world, which had only recently gained the upper hand and declared Yahweh dead, are deposed from their thrones overnight. They pass away, but he remains. He "is". His "I am" is not only the present reality of God; it is also his constancy. In every transition he is present; yesterday, today, tomorrow. Eternity is not the past. It is this absolute reliability and constancy that always bears us up. God "is": this touches us in a new manner in an age in which we tend very often to confuse what is up to date with what is good, what is modern with what is true. But time is not God. God is the Eternal; where time is worshipped, it is an idol.[5]

At this point, we must ask an even more fundamental and general question: What does it mean to speak of a "name of God"? When God receives names in the Old Testament, can this be anything more than a reminiscence of the polytheistic world in which Israel's faith in God was obliged to struggle step by step to find its own form? This view may seem to find support in the fact that the individual names of God, which are numerous in the early strata

[5] Cf. J. Ratzinger, *Dogma und Verkündigung* (Munich, 1973), pp. 407ff.

of the tradition, disappear gradually, as the Old Testament faith develops; although the name "Yahweh" is retained, the Second Commandment meant that it had ceased to be uttered long before the time of Jesus. The New Testament no longer knows any proper name of God; one contributory factor here was the fact that in the Greek Old Testament, the name "Yahweh" had already been largely replaced by the term "Lord". But this is only one aspect of the matter. It is indeed true that the individual names of God disappear once the polytheistic beginnings are left behind; but it is also true that the idea that God has a name plays a decisive role precisely in the New Testament. In many ways, one may regard the seventeenth chapter of John's Gospel as the high point of the development of the New Testament faith, and this brief text speaks four times of "the name of God". The principal part of the text, in verses 6 and 26, is set within the framework of Jesus' testimony to his own mission, which consists in making known to men the name of God. Jesus appears here as the new Moses who now accomplishes completely and in reality what had begun in a fragmentary and hidden manner at the burning bush in the wilderness.

What, then, does "the name of God" mean? Perhaps it is easiest to grasp what this entails if we look at its opposite. The Revelation of John speaks of the adversary of God, the "beast". This beast, the power opposed to God, has no name, but a number. The seer tells us: "Its number is six hundred and sixty-six" (13:18). It is a number, and it makes men numbers. We who lived through the world of the concentration camps know what that means. The terror of that world is rooted in the fact that it obliterates men's faces. It obliterates their history. It makes man a number, an exchangeable cog in one big machine. He is his function—nothing more. Today, we must fear that the concentration camp was only a prelude and that the universal law of the machine may impose the structure of the concentration camp on the world as a whole. For when functions are all that exist, man, too, is nothing more than a function. The machines that he himself has constructed now impose their own law on him: he must be made readable for the computer, and this can be achieved only when he is translated into numbers. Everything else in man becomes irrelevant. Whatever is not a function is—nothing. The beast is a number, and it makes men numbers. But God has a name, and God calls us by our name. He is a Person, and he seeks the person. He has a face, and he seeks our face. He has a heart, and he seeks our heart. For him, we are not some function in a "world machinery". On the contrary, it is precisely those who have no function who are his own. A name allows me to be addressed. A name denotes community. This is why Christ is the true Moses, the fulfillment of the revelation of God's name. He does not bring some new word as God's name; he does more than this, since he himself is the face of God. He himself is the name of God. In him, we can address God as "you", as person, as heart. His own name, Jesus, brings the mysterious name at the burning bush to its fulfillment; now we can see that God had not said all that he had to say but had interrupted his discourse for a time. This is because the name "Jesus" in its Hebrew form includes the word "Yahweh" and adds a further element to it: God "saves". "I am who I am"—thanks to Jesus, this now means: "I am the one who saves you." His Being is salvation.

In the Church's calendar, today (March 8) is the feast of Saint John "of God", the founder of the Hospitaller Brothers, who continue even today to care for the sick. From the time of his conversion onward, the life of this man was a continuous pouring out of himself for other people, for the suffering and the rejected, as well as for those who were poorest of all at that time, the mentally ill and prostitutes, for whom he sought to make a new life possible. The letters he wrote give a striking impression of the passion with which this man was consumed for the oppressed. "I work here on borrowed money, a prisoner for the sake of Jesus Christ. And often my debts are so pressing that I dare not go out of the house for fear of being seized by my creditors. Whenever I see so many poor brothers and neighbors of mine suffering beyond their strength and overwhelmed with so many physical or mental ills which I cannot alleviate, then I become exceedingly sorrowful; but I trust in Christ, who knows my heart."[6] I find it profoundly significant that this man was given the sobriquet "of God". In this life, totally spent in the service of men, we see in an incomparable manner who God is—the God of the burning bush, the God of Jesus Christ, he who is the right of those who have no rights, he who is eternal and close at hand; he who has names and who gives names. May we, too, be ever more "of God", so that we may have an ever-deeper knowledge of God and become for others a path to the knowledge of God.

---

[6] Quoted from the Office of Readings in the Liturgy of the Hours on the feast of the saint; cf. O. Marcos, *Cartos y escritos de Nuestro Glorioso Padre San Juan de Dios* (Madrid, 1935). Cf. the brief presentation of his life by H. Firtel, in P. Manns, *Die Heiligen* (Mainz, 1975), pp. 481–84. My reference to John of God goes back to the specific situation in which I was preaching. I have consciously retained it here as a narrative that adds concrete details to my preceding remarks.

# God is three and God is one

How often have we made the sign of the Cross and invoked the name of the triune God without thinking about what we were doing? In its original meaning, each time we perform this action, our baptism is renewed. We take on our lips the words through which we were made Christians, and we consciously accept into our personal life something that was bestowed on us in baptism without any active contribution or reflection on our part. On that occasion, water was poured over us, and the following words were spoken: "I baptize you in the name of the Father and of the Son and of the Holy Spirit." The Church makes a man a Christian by pronouncing the name of the triune God. In this way, she has expressed since the very beginning what she considers the most decisive element of the Christian existence, namely, faith in the triune God.

This disappoints us. It is so far removed from our life. It is so useless and so incomprehensible. If some brief formula must be used, then we expect something attractive and exciting, something that immediately strikes us as important for man and for his life. And yet the essential point is precisely what is stated here: the primary concern in Christianity is, not the Church or man, but God. Christianity is oriented, not to our own hopes, fears, and needs, but to God, to his sovereignty and power. The first proposition of the Christian faith and the fundamental orientation of Christian conversion is: "God is."

But what does this mean? What does it mean in our daily life in this world of ours? Let us begin by saying that

God exists and, consequently, that the "gods" are not God. Accordingly, we must worship him, no one else. But, one might ask, are not the gods long since dead anyway? Is this not perfectly obvious and, hence, an empty affirmation? But one who looks attentively at reality must counter this response with a question of his own: Has idolatry really ceased in our day? Is there really no longer anything that is worshipped alongside God and against God? Is it not rather the case that, after the "death of God", the gods are ascending once more from the depths with a terrible power?

Martin Luther offered an impressive formulation of this reality in his *Large Catechism*: "What does it mean to have a god, or what is god? *Answer*: A god means that from which we are to expect every good and to which we are to take refuge in every distress, so that to have a god is nothing else than to trust and believe him from the heart; as I have often said that the confidence and faith of the heart alone make both God and an idol."[7] In what, then, do we place our trust? In what do we believe? Have not money, power, prestige, public opinion, and sex become powers before which men bow down and which they serve like gods? Would not the world look different if these gods were to be deposed from their throne?

God is—and, therefore, that which is true and right is superior to all our goals and interests. That which is worthless in earthly terms has a worth. The adoration of God himself, true adoration, exists, protecting man from the dictatorship of goals. Only this adoration is able to protect him from the dictatorship of idols.

---

[7] *Triglot Concordia: The Symbolical Books of the Evangelical Lutheran Church*, trans. F. Bente and W. H. Dau (St. Louis, 1921), pp. 565ff. The problematic nature of this text is exposed acutely by P. Hacker, *Das Ich im Glauben bei Martin Luther* (Graz, 1966), pp. 21ff., but we need not discuss this in the present context.

God is—and this also means that all of us are his creatures. Only creatures, indeed; but precisely because we are
creatures, we have our true origin in God. We are creatures whom he has willed and whom he has destined for
eternity. This is also true of my neighbor, the one beside
me whom I may not find at all attractive. Man is not the
product of chance. He is not the outcome of a mere struggle for existence that ensures the victory of that which
conforms to some goal or other or of that which is able
to get its way at the expense of others. No, man owes his
origin to God's creative love.

God is—and here we must underline that little word
*is*. For God truly is: in other words, he is at work, he
acts, and he can act. He is not a remote origin, nor is
he some indeterminate "goal of our transcending". He has
not abdicated in favor of his world-machine; he has not
lost his own function in a world where everything would
function autonomously without him. No, the world is
and remains *his* world. The present is his time—not the
past. He can act, and he does act in a very real way now,
in this world and in our life. Do we trust him? When we
make plans for our life, for our day-to-day existence, do
we see him as a reality? Have we understood the meaning
of the first table of the Ten Commandments, which is
the truly fundamental challenge to human life, in keeping
with the first three requests of the Lord's Prayer, which
take up this first table and seek to make it the fundamental
orientation of our spirit and our life?

God is—and the Christian faith adds: God is as Father,
Son, and Holy Spirit, three and one. This is the very heart
of Christianity, but it is so often shrouded in a silence
born of perplexity. Has the Church perhaps gone one
step too far here? Ought we not rather leave something
so great and inaccessible as God in his inaccessibility? Can

something like the Trinity have any real meaning for us? Well, it is certainly true that the proposition that "God is three and God is one" is and remains the expression of his otherness, which is infinitely greater than we and transcends all our thinking and our existence. But if this proposition had nothing to say to us, it would not have been revealed. And, as a matter of fact, it could be clothed in human language only because it had already penetrated human thinking and living to some extent.

What, then, does this mean? Let us begin at the point where God himself began. He calls himself Father. Human fatherhood can give us an inkling of what God is; but where fatherhood no longer exists, where genuine fatherhood is no longer experienced as a phenomenon that goes beyond the biological dimension to embrace a human and intellectual sphere as well, it becomes meaningless to speak of God the Father. Where human fatherhood disappears, it is no longer possible to speak and think of God. It is not God who is dead; what is dead (at least to a large extent) is the precondition in man that makes it possible for God to live in the world. The crisis of fatherhood that we are experiencing today is a basic aspect of the crisis that threatens mankind as a whole. Where fatherhood is perceived only as a biological accident on which no genuinely human claims may be based, or the father is seen as a tyrant whose yoke must be thrown off, something in the basic structure of human existence has been damaged. If human existence is to be complete, we need a father, in the true meaning of fatherhood that our faith discloses, namely, a responsibility for one's child that does not dominate him but permits him to become his own self. This fatherhood is a love that avoids two traps: the total subjugation of the child to the father's own priorities and goals, on the one hand, and the unquestioning acceptance of the child as he is, under the pretext that this is the expression of freedom, on the other. Responsibility for one's child means the desire that he realize his own innermost truth, which lies in his Creator. And naturally, a fatherhood of this kind is possible only if one accepts one's own status as a child. If men are to be fathers in the correct way, they must assent in their heart to the words of Jesus: "You have [only] one Father, who is heaven" (Mt 23:9). This has nothing to do with a domination that makes others one's slaves. It is a responsibility born of truth: because I have freely handed myself over to God, I can now free the other to be himself, without egoism, free for the God in whom he has his existence.

Here, of course, another point is important: the fact that the primary biblical image of God is the "Father" also means that the mystery of motherhood, too, has its origin in him and has exactly the same potential as fatherhood either to point to God or, when it is distorted, to point away from him. Here we can grasp what it means in real and very practical terms to affirm that man is "the image of God". Man is not God's image as an abstraction—for that would lead in turn only to an abstract God. He is God's image in his concrete reality, which is relationship: he is God's image as father, as mother, as child ("son"). This means that when we apply these words to God, they are "images"; but they are images precisely because man is an "image", and therein lies their claim to reality. They are images that require "the Image", and this means that they can be the realization of God or his "death". We cannot separate man's becoming man and his knowledge of God precisely because he is "the image" of God. When his humanity is destroyed, something happens to the image of God. The dissolution of fatherhood and motherhood, which some would prefer to relocate in a laboratory[8] or at least reduce to a biological moment that does not concern man *qua* man, is linked to the dissolution of childhood, which must give way to a total equality from the very beginning. This is a program of hubris, which at one and the same time wants to remove man from the biological sphere and enslaves him completely within it; this hubris reaches into the very roots of human existence and into the roots of the ability to think of God, for where he can no longer be depicted in an image, it is no longer possible to think of him. Where human thought employs all its power to make it impossible to depict God in an image, no "proof of God's existence" can ever have anything to say.

Naturally, we must not indulge in wild exaggerations when we criticize the age in which we live. To begin with, we must not forget that there are exemplary fathers and mothers even today and that great figures such as Janusc Korczak and Mother Teresa demonstrate in our age that the reality of fatherhood and motherhood can be achieved even without the biological dimension. Besides this, we must always remember that the utterly pure realization of the image of God has always been an exception: God's image in man has always been stained and distorted. This is why it is empty romanticism to plead: "Spare us the dogmas, the Christology, the Holy Spirit, the Trinity! It suffices to proclaim God as Father and all men as brothers and to live this without any mystical theories. That is the only thing that matters!" This sounds very plausible, but does this really do justice to the complicated being called man? How do we know what fatherhood is or what it means to be brothers and sisters? What entitles us to put so

---

[8] [This text was written several years before the birth of the first "test-tube baby" in England in 1978.—TRANS.]

much trust in these realities? There are indeed moving testimonies in early cultures to a pure trust in the "Father" in the skies, but subsequent development mostly meant that religious attention very quickly moved away from him to concentrate on "powers" that were much closer at hand; in the course of history, the image of man, and hence also the image of God, everywhere took on ambiguous traits. It is well known that the Greeks called their Zeus "Father". But this word was not an expression of their trust in him! Rather, it expressed the profound ambiguity of the god and the tragic ambiguity, indeed, the terrible character, of the world. When they said "Father", they meant that Zeus was like human fathers—sometimes really nice, when he was in a good mood, but ultimately an egoist, a tyrant, unpredictable, unfathomable, and dangerous. And this was how they experienced the dark power that ruled the world: some individuals are courted as favorites, but this power stands by indifferently while other individuals starve to death, are enslaved, or go to ruin. The "Father" of the world, as he is experienced in human life, reflects human fathers: partisan and, in the last analysis, terrible.

People today bid farewell to the world of the fathers and sing the enthusiastic praises of "brotherhood". But in our de facto experience, is brotherhood really so unambiguous, so full of hope? According to the Bible, the first pair of brothers in world history were Cain and Abel; in Roman myth, we find the corresponding pair of Romulus and Remus. This motif is found everywhere and is a cruel parody—but one written by reality itself—of the hymn to "brotherhood". Have not our experiences since 1789 contributed new and even more dreadful features to this parody? Have they not confirmed the vision that bears the name "Cain and Abel" rather than what the word "brotherhood" promised us?

How, then, do we know that fatherhood is a kindness on which we can rely and that God, despite all outward appearances, is not playing with the world, but loves it dependably? For this, it was necessary that God should show himself, overthrow the images, and set up a new criterion. This takes place in the Son, in Christ. In his prayer, he plunges the totality of his life into the abyss of truth and of goodness that is God. It is only on the basis of this Son that we truly experience what God is. The nineteenth-century critics of religion claimed that the religions came into being when men projected their own best and most beautiful characteristics onto heaven, in order to make the world bearable for themselves; but since they were only projecting something of their own selves onto heaven, this took the name of Zeus and was terrible. The biblical Father is not a heavenly duplicate of human fatherhood. Rather, he posits something new: he is the divine critique of human fatherhood. God establishes his own criterion.[9]

Without Jesus, we do not know what "Father" truly is. This becomes visible in his prayer, which is the foundation of his being. A Jesus who was not continuously absorbed in the Father and was not in continuous intimate communication with him would be a completely different being from the Jesus of the Bible, the real Jesus of history. Prayer was the center out of which he lived, and it was prayer that showed him how to understand God, the world, and men. To follow Jesus means looking at the world with the eyes of God and living accordingly. Jesus shows us what it means to lead the whole of one's life on the basis of the affirmation that "God is." Jesus shows us what it means to give genuine priority to the first table of the Ten

---

[9] The following passage is closely dependent on my remarks in *Dogma und Verkündigung*, pp. 101–4 and 94–98.

Commandments. He gave this center a meaning, and he revealed what this center is.

At this point, however, a question arises. Jesus lives in an uninterrupted prayerful communication with God, which is the foundation of his existence. Without this, he would not be the one he is. But is this communication equally essential to the Father whom he addresses, in the sense that the Father, too, would be someone else if he were not addressed in this way? Or does this prayer pass him by without penetrating him? The answer is that it is just as essential to the Father to say "Son" as it is essential to the Son to say "Father". Without this address, the Father, too, would not be the same. Jesus does not merely touch him from the outside; he belongs to the divinity of God, as Son. Before the world was made, God is already the love of Father and Son. He can become our Father and the criterion of all fatherhood precisely because he himself is Father from eternity. In Jesus' prayer, the inner life of God becomes visible to us: we see how God himself is. Faith in the triune God is nothing other than the exposition of what takes place in Jesus' prayer. In his prayer, the Trinity is revealed.

The next question is: "Why a Trinity? We have grasped that God is two—after what you have said, this makes perfect sense. But where does this third Person suddenly come from?"

I will devote a meditation specifically to this question; here, I simply wish to indicate where the answer lies. It is impossible for a mere "twofoldness" to exist. Either the contraposition, that is, the fact that there are *two*, will endure, so that no genuine unity comes about; or else the two will melt into each other, so that they are no longer *genuinely* two. Let me try to put this in less abstract terms. The Father and the Son do not become one in such a way that they dissolve into each other. They remain distinct from each other, since love has its basis in a "vis-à-vis" that is not abolished. If each remains his own self, and they do not abrogate each other's existence, then their unity cannot exist in each one by himself: rather, their unity must be in the fruitfulness in which each one gives himself and in which each one is himself. They are one in virtue of the fact that their love is fruitful, that it goes beyond them. In the third Person in whom they give themselves to each other, in the Gift, they are themselves, and they are one.

Let us return to my earlier point: in Jesus' prayer, the Father becomes visible and Jesus makes himself known as the Son. The unity that this reveals is the Trinity. Accordingly, becoming a Christian means sharing in Jesus' prayer, entering into the model provided by his life, that is, the model of his prayer. Becoming a Christian means saying "Father" with Jesus and, thus, becoming a child, God's son—God—in the unity of the Spirit, who allows us to be ourselves and precisely in this way draws us into the unity of God. Being a Christian means looking at the world from this central point, which gives us freedom, hope, decisiveness, and consolation.

This brings us back to the starting point of these reflections. We were baptized in the name of the Father, the Son, and the Holy Spirit before we knew what was happening to us. Today, many people doubt whether this is a good thing. We have the impression that decisions are being anticipated and imposed on the person that only he himself can properly make. Such presumption seems to us a questionable limitation on human freedom in a central sphere of life.

Such feelings express our profound uncertainty with regard to the Christian faith itself. We find it a burden rather than a grace—a burden that one may accept only for oneself. But here we are forgetting that life, too, is something determined in advance for us—we are not consulted beforehand! And life entails so much else as well: when a person is born, not only his biological existence is determined in advance, but also his language, the age in which he lives, its way of thinking, its evaluations. A life without "advance gifts" of this kind does not exist; the question is *what* these advance gifts are. If baptism establishes the "advance gift" of being loved by eternal Love, could any gift be more precious and pure than this? The advance gift of life alone is meaningless and can become a terrible burden. May we determine in advance the life another person is to lead? This is defensible only if life itself is defensible, that is, when life is sustained by a hope that goes beyond all the terrors of earthly existence.[10]

Where the Church is regarded only as an accidental human association, the "advance gift" of faith will be questionable. But one who is convinced that it is a question, not of some human association, but rather of the gift of the love that already awaits us even before we draw our first breath will see his most precious task as the preparation of another person to receive the advance gift of love—for it is only *this* gift that justifies passing on the gift of life to him. This means that we must learn anew to take God as our starting point when we seek to understand the Christian existence. This existence is belief in his love and faith that he is Father, Son, and Holy Spirit—for it is only thus that the affirmation that he is "love" becomes meaningful. If he is not love in himself, he is not love at all. But if he is love in himself, he must be "I" and "Thou", and

---

[10] I have set out these arguments in greater detail and justified my position in my essay "Taufe, Glaube und Zugehörigkeit zur Kirche", *Internationale katholische Zeitschrift* 5 (1976): 218–34, esp. 232ff.

this means that he must be triune. Let us ask him to open our eyes so that he becomes once again the basis of our understanding of the Christian existence, for in this way we shall understand ourselves anew and renew mankind.

# The Creator God

In his Hassidic stories, Martin Buber writes about the first visit paid by the future Rabbi Levi Yitzhak to Rabbi Schmelke of Nikolsburg. His desire for a deeper knowledge of ultimate reality was so strong that he undertook this journey against the wishes of his father-in-law, and on his return, his father-in-law demanded imperiously: "Well, what did you learn from him?" Levi Yitzhak replied: "I have learned that there is a Creator of the world." The old man called his servant and asked him: "Are you aware that there is a Creator of the world?" "Yes", said the servant. Levi Yitzhak exclaimed, "Naturally, everyone *says* that. But do they also learn it?"[11] In this meditation, let us attempt to "learn" somewhat more deeply what it means to say that God is Creator.

What, then, does it mean? First of all, it means that the Christian faith concerns the whole of reality. It concerns reason. It asks a question that concerns everyone. By now, proofs of the existence of God have been declared dead even in theology. It is indeed correct to say that they were often set out too superficially, without paying sufficient attention to their anchoring in the deeper questions that we have discussed in our first two meditations. It is also correct to say that these proofs were not always presented with true intellectual rigor, and we must also note that the word "proof" has acquired a meaning in scientific

[11] M. Buber, *Schriften zum Chassidismus*, vol. 3 of *Werke* (Munich and Heidelberg, 1963), p. 323.

thinking that it certainly cannot have in this context. In this sense, a corrective was certainly necessary. If, however, we were to declare obsolete the very intention of these "proofs", this would have very grave consequences, since we would thereby deprive the faith of its opening to the sphere of that reason which is shared by all men. Where this happens, faith shrinks to the status of one specific phenomenon. It is then only one of the many traditions of mankind—some have this tradition, while others cultivate another tradition. Instead of being truth, it becomes folklore. Before, the faith possessed an obligatory character that was inherently justified; now, it is merely a product that the salesman must implore his customers to buy. No one can find any joy in such a faith, since joy in the faith is decisively dependent on the knowledge that it is not just anything but is the precious pearl of truth.

And yet, the transparency of the world to the Creator ought to be greater today than ever before. Today, we understand that what seemed in the past to be dead matter is an entity full of spirit. The more we penetrate into the depths of the structures of solid matter, the "mass", the more full of holes it becomes; under our very eyes, the "mass" eludes our grasp. All the more triumphantly, however, does the spirit emerge, and when we see the interconnections between the hidden structures, this both shames and inspires our own spirit. In his conversations with his friends, Heisenberg strikingly observed that another process ran parallel to the formation of modern physics, namely, the end of a positivist, self-imposed moderation that made the question of God off-limits to physicists. He shows how the knowledge of reality and of its depths compelled physicists to inquire into the order that sustains it. To begin with, these conversations employ the term "central order" to refer to what was once meant by the word "God".[12] The true substance that lies hidden behind this cautiously groping concept comes to light when it is no longer possible to avoid asking whether this order can assert itself beyond the fact of its mere existence, whether it possesses a quality that must be thought of as analogous to that of the human person: "We cannot doubt the existence of the central order of things or of events. Can you or can one encounter this order with the same immediacy, make contact with it with the same immediacy as is possible with the soul of another man? ... If you put the question in these terms, I would answer Yes."[13] Heisenberg does not hesitate to link the question of the "central order" with the question of the "compass" that we ought to follow when we seek our path through life.[14] The very concept of a central order points to something like a "compass", which both makes demands and provides a criterion; hence it is only logical that Heisenberg is not afraid to draw a very concrete conclusion (which of course leads far beyond his starting point in the observation of the order of the world), namely, that the Christian faith is the word of encouragement that this central order addresses to us. "When once the magnetic power that has guided this compass is completely extinguished—and the power can come only from the central order—then I fear that very terrible things can happen, far surpassing the concentration camps and the atomic bombs."[15]

[12] W. Heisenberg, *Der Teil und das Ganze* (Munich, 1969), pp. 118, 293ff.

[13] Ibid., p. 293.

[14] Ibid., pp. 291, 294.

[15] Ibid., p. 295. On this whole question, cf. my essay "Ich glaube an Gott den Vater, den Allmächtigen, den Schöpfer des Himmels und der Erde", in *Ich glaube: Vierzehn Betrachtungen zum Apostolischen Glaubensbekenntnis*, ed. W. Sandfuchs, pp. 13–24 (Würzburg, 1975).

I have anticipated my conclusions here. The Christian faith is not opposed to reason. It protects reason and its questions about the totality of things. Until recently, faith was often accused of being hostile to progress and of kindling an unhealthy resentment vis-à-vis technology. Today, now that it has become fashionable to have one's doubts about the blessings of technology, we hear exactly the opposite accusation: with its maxim "Subdue the earth!" and its de-divinization of the world, the Christian faith has generated the attitude of an unchecked domination and exploitation of the earth, thereby creating the curse of technology. We need not discuss here the extent to which individual Christians may have incurred guilt in one or other of these directions; the important point is that *both* accusations interpret wrongly the thrust of faith itself. It is true that faith hands the world over to man and is thus one of the factors that made the modern age possible. But faith always links the question of domination over the world to the question of creation by God and of the meaning of this creation. Faith makes technical research and questioning possible because it explains the rational character of the world and the orientation of the world toward man; but it is profoundly opposed to restricting thought exclusively to questions of function and usefulness. Faith challenges man to look beyond immediate usefulness and to ask about the foundations of the totality of things. Faith protects the contemplative and listening reason from attack by the merely instrumental reason.

This brings us to our next point. Faith in God's creation is not concerned with mere theory or with the question about a very distant past in which the world came into being. This faith is concerned about the present, about the correct attitude vis-à-vis reality. For Christian faith in the creation, it is decisively important that the Creator

and the Redeemer, the God of the origin and the God
of the end, be one and the same. Where this unity is dissolved, the result is "heresy", and the basic form of the
faith itself disintegrates. The forms in which this temptation appears always make it seem totally new, but it is in
fact extremely ancient. At the beginning of Church history, Marcion from Asia Minor was the first to clothe this
temptation in a fascinating form. The universal Church
affirmed the unity between Jesus and the Old Testament,
but Marcion objected that since the New Testament
explicitly stated that the Jews did not know the Father of
Jesus Christ, that is, his God, the God of the Old Testament could not be the God of Jesus Christ: Jesus brought
a genuinely new God who had been unknown up to that
point, one who had nothing in common with the jealous,
wrathful, avenging God of the Old Covenant. *His* God
was only love, forgiveness, and joy; his God no longer
uttered threats, but was pure hope and forgiveness. Only
he was the "good God". Jesus came in order to free man
from the law of the old God and from the old God himself
and to entrust him to the God of grace who appeared in
Jesus himself. The denial of the old God, which Marcion
announces in these terms, is at the same time a denial of his
"unsuccessful" creation, a rebellion against the creation in
favor of a new world.[16]

Anyone who follows today's intellectual developments
attentively can observe that one might speak of a return of
Marcion in many ways. There are of course differences,
and it is these that the superficial observer is usually quick

[16] H. Rahner, "Markion", in *Lexikon für Theologie und Kirche*, 2nd ed., 7,
cols. 92f., provides general information about Marcion; cf. also J. Quasten,
*Patrology* 1 (Utrecht and Westminster, Md., 1962), pp. 268–72. The basic
monograph remains A. Harnack, *Marcion: Das Evangelium vom fremden Gott*,
2nd ed. (Leipzig and Berlin, 1924); cf. also Harnack, *Neue Studien zu Marcion*
(Leipzig and Berlin, 1923).

to notice. He can point out that Marcion's disavowal of the creation led him to a truly neurotic hostility to the body, something we find very alien. It was typical of the "dark Middle Ages" and was inherited by the universal Church, but precisely this is being overcome today. One can of course question whether it would have been possible to build such cathedrals and compose such music if there had not been a deep love for the creation, for matter, and for the body; but a scholarly dispute of that kind would not touch the heart of the matter. The truth is that the rejection of Creator and creation, which Marcion shares with the wide stream of so-called gnosis, generated not only an ascetical contempt for the body, but also a cynical libertinism, for this too displays in reality a hatred of the body, of man, and of the world. These two apparent extremes lie very close to one another, and their basic attitudes overlap. In the false asceticism that is hostile to the creation, the body becomes a dirty bag of maggots that deserves only disdain or, indeed, ill treatment. Similarly, the basic principle underlying libertinism is the degradation of the body to a mere thing. Its exclusion from the realm of ethics and of the mind's responsibility means its exclusion from that which makes man human, its exclusion from the dignity of the spirit. It becomes a mere object, a thing, and thus the life of man, too, becomes cheap and common. Have we not, then, rejoined Marcion, starting from the other end? And do we not find refined forms of such an exclusion of the body from the realm of the human, with its reduction to a thing and hence to an object of contempt, even in theology? Is it not the case here, too, that God is no longer permitted to have anything to do with the body, so that every genuine inclusion of the bodily sphere in the question of the Virgin Birth or in the profession of faith in the Lord's Resurrection is dismissed as unenlightened naïveté? Is not the idea that God could become so concrete, so material, rejected with an indignant wrinkling of the brow?

But we have not yet grasped the full significance of this idea. Where man despises his body—whether as an ascetic or as a libertine—he also despises his own self. Both an asceticism hostile to the creation and libertinism lead man by an inherent necessity to hate this life of his, to hate himself, indeed, to hate reality as a whole, and herein lies the explosive political power of both these basic attitudes. A man who feels himself disgraced in this way would like to tear apart this prison of shame, that is, his body and the world, in order to escape from such a humiliation. He cries out for another world because he hates the creation and the God who bears responsibility for all this.

This is why gnosis, for the very first time in the history of the mind, became an ideology of total revolution.[17] Something much more fundamental is at stake here than political or social power struggles, which have always existed: here we find a rage directed against reality itself, which man has learned to hate in the course of his own muddled existence. When he despises his body, man quarrels on a radical level with Being itself, which he understands, no longer as God's creation, but as "the existing order", which must be destroyed. In the ideology of revolution, Marx and Marcion are terribly close to one another. This is why the revolution is transformed from a political instrument into a religious idol. It is no longer an attack on some specific political situation, but a struggle between two kinds of "god", a rebellion against reality itself, which is the "existing order" that must be trampled underfoot in order to create space for something completely different.

---

[17] On the revolutionary character of gnosis, cf. H. Jonas, *Gnosis und spätantiker Geist* 1 and 2/1, 2nd ed. (Göttingen, 1954); E. Voegelin, *Wissenschaft, Politik und Gnosis* (Munich, 1959).

And this is why the debate about ethical values is never a dispute confined to moral questions alone: it is always a metaphysical conflict, a dispute about Being itself. When the existence of the family, and thereby the human reality of fatherhood and motherhood, is defamed as an alleged hindrance to freedom; when honesty, obedience, fidelity, patience, kindness, and trust are portrayed as inventions of the ruling classes, and our children are taught hatred, mistrust, and disobedience (since these are the true virtues of the man who liberates himself)—then the Creator himself and his creation are at stake, for the intention is the complete replacement of his creation by another world that man will build for himself. The logic of this position means that only hatred can really be the path to love; but this logic itself is the consequence of the anti-logic of self-destruction, since where reality as a whole is slandered and the Creator is scorned, man cuts off the roots of his own self. We are beginning to recognize this in a very palpable manner on a much lower level, in the environmental question, where we see that man cannot live *against* the earth for the simple reason that he must live *from* the earth. But we are not yet ready to accept that this principle applies to the entire spectrum of reality.

These reflections have illustrated, step by step, what I said above when I took up Heisenberg's remarks without at that point arguing in detail for their correctness: namely, that the creation is not only something that concerns the theoretical reason, something we see and admire. The creation is a "compass".[18] In the past, people spoke of a

---

[18] On the implications of the theology of the creation, which are only suggested here, cf. the acute analysis by P. Schmidt, "Ich glaube an Gott, den Schöpfer des Himmels und der Erde", *Internationale katholische Zeitschrift* 5 (1976): 1–14; G. Martelet, "Der Erstgeborene aller Schöpfung", *Internationale katholische Zeitschrift* 5 (1976): 15–29; and R. Buttiglione and A. Scola, "Von Abraham zu Prometheus", *Internationale katholische Zeitschrift* 5 (1976): 30–41.

natural law. Today, this idea has become a laughingstock, and it is doubtless true that it has often been misused in the past; nevertheless, the kernel still holds good. There exists something that is "naturally" right, thanks to the compass provided by the creation, something that makes possible an international law that transcends the boundaries of those laws that are promulgated by individual states. There exists something that is naturally right, antecedent to our legislation, and hence it is simply impossible for *everything* that occurs to men to be "right". It is possible for laws to exist that are indeed valid legal statutes but are in fact injustice rather than "justice". Since it is God's creation, nature itself is a source of law. It indicates boundaries that must not be transgressed. The immediate relevance of this question is obvious: where the killing of innocent life is declared to be a "right", injustice is made a law. Where the rule of law no longer protects human life, it is questionable whether it deserves the name of law. In saying this, I do not intend to impose a specifically Christian morality on all the citizens in a pluralistic society; no, what is involved here is *humanitas*, the "specifically human quality" of man, who cannot declare the trampling underfoot of creation to be his own liberation without deceiving himself on a very profound level. The passion with which this debate is conducted is due to the profundity of the question at issue: Is man free only once he has unchained himself from the creation and left it behind, as something that enslaved him? Or does he not thereby deny his own self? Ultimately, this controversy is about man himself, and a Christian cannot dispense himself from taking part in this debate by saying that it is pointless since the others do not share his own moral values. That would be to misunderstand the true significance of the question. It would also be to misunderstand the true significance of the Christian message, which is more than the ethos of one particular group. It is a responsibility for man as a whole, precisely thanks to the fact that his Redeemer is none other than his Creator.

At this point, we can see another aspect that is characteristic of man's situation today. Is there not a profound fear of the future in the great pains people take to block the path to new human life? This fear seems to have two elements. First of all, it surely is based on a feeling that the gift of life is not meaningful, because we can no longer see God's gift of meaning. Here, we see a despair at one's own life, which generates a reluctance to impose on others the dark path of life. Secondly, it is clear that there is also a simple fear of competition, the fear of the limitation that the other person would surely impose on me. The other one, that is, the child who would be born, becomes a danger. True love is an event of dying, a stepping aside before the other and on behalf of the other. We do not want to die like that. We just want to remain ourselves, enjoying life to the full, without any disturbance and without sharing it with anyone else. We do not perceive, nor do we want to perceive, that we are destroying our own future through our greed for life and handing over our life itself to death.

And here we see one final point: belief in the Creator God is also belief in the God of our conscience. Because he is the Creator, he is close to each one of us in our conscience. The very personal content of the profession of faith in the Creator comes to light in our faith in the conscience. Conscience is higher than the law: it makes a distinction between those laws that are just and those that are unjust. Conscience means the priority of the truth. And this means that the conscience is not an arbitrary principle but an expression of belief in the secret knowledge shared between man and the truth. In our conscience, we are confidants of the truth. At the same time, our conscience challenges us to search ever more earnestly for the truth.

I believe in God the Creator. Let us ask him that we may "learn" what this means.

# Job's question

The image of God is man. The God of the Old Covenant tolerates no other image. In the holy of holies of the Temple there is no statue of the divinity, as in the temples of the other peoples, but only the empty throne that contains the tables with his Word and the vessel with the manna.[19] This is his image: the empty throne that points to his infinite sovereignty and power; his Word, the expression of his holiness, which desires to dwell in man; his bread, the sign of his power over creation and history, the sign of his goodness that imparts life to the creatures to whom he has given the world as their home. All this points to man. He is meant to be God's throne and the place of his Word; he lives from the goodness of the creation and of him who made it. Man is God's image—and only man.

When we reflect more deeply on this, we can be assailed by a dreadful feeling. There are, indeed, many blessed moments in which something of God becomes visible through man: in the great works of art that have been given to man in his history, we sense something of God's creative imagination, something of the Creator Spirit and of his eternal beauty that transcends every word and all the calculations of logic. More than this, and on an

[19] This is how Hebrews 9:4 describes the furnishings of the holy of holies. On the complicated question of its actual historical form in the various stages of the Temple, the most important material is presented by A. van den Born and W. Baier, "Allerheiligstes", in *Bibellexikon*, ed. H. Haag, 2nd ed., p. 48 (Einsiedeln, 1968).

even deeper level, we sense something of God himself in the kindness of someone who is simply good, someone who does not ask why he should be good or what he will get out of it. An eyewitness once told me about some Asian girls who had experienced much distress and were then taken in by nuns who looked after them. These girls addressed the sisters as "God", because they said that no human being could be capable of such kindness.

Thanks be to God, there is a transparency to God through people. But our experience is much more strongly marked by the opposite. In his history, man so often seems to prove the existence of a demon (or at least of an ambiguous being) rather than of a good God. Man disproves the existence of the God to whom the creation points. Perhaps this is the real reason why the "proofs of God" are always ultimately ineffective: the light that penetrates through the seams of the creation is blocked by man. We need not recall such terrible names as Nero, Hitler, or Stalin; it suffices to think of our own experiences with other people and with our own selves.

In addition to all the guilt of man, with all the darkness this generates, there is the incomprehensible suffering of the innocent—the most terrible accusation that rises up against God in the ever-harsher tones of a chorus that reaches from Job to Dostoevsky and Auschwitz. Job cannot accept the apologia for God with which his friends attempt to explain his suffering; but this apologia is nothing other than the hitherto valid wisdom of Israel, which interpreted suffering as the punishment for sin and prosperity as the reward for good conduct. The world thus appeared as a structure of reward and punishment, organized in a system of strict justice (even if we are not always able to discern the reasons behind this justice). Job rebels with all the passion of the tortured innocent man against such an image of God, since his own experience is completely different: God "destroys both the blameless and the wicked. When disaster brings sudden death, he mocks at the calamity of the innocent. The earth is given into the hand of the wicked; he covers the face of its judges—if it is not he, who then is it?" (9:22–24). He counters the wonderful song of the confidence that knows it is kept safe in the ubiquitous presence of God (Ps 139 [138])[20] with the opposite experience (23:8f.):

Behold, I go forward, but he is not there;
    and backward, but I cannot perceive him;
on the left hand I seek him, but I cannot behold him;
    I turn to the right hand, but I cannot see him.

This experience shatters the original joy in life (10:18):

Why did you bring me forth from the womb?
    Would that I had died before any eye had seen me.

Behind Job's cry stand today the millions who perished namelessly in the gas chambers of Auschwitz and in the prisons of dictatorships of the left and the right. The accusers shout ever more loudly: "Where is your God?" No doubt, such words are often an expression of cynicism rather than of genuine respect in the face of the terrible character of human suffering. But the lamentation is true. Where are you, God? Who are you, that you keep silent?

Only God himself can reply. He has not done so in a conclusive manner. He has not done it in such a way that one could lay the answer on one's desk and check the calculations. But nor has he been completely silent.

---

[20] Cf. my remarks in the first meditation, above, p. 28.

It is true that his final word has not yet been spoken; in the Resurrection of Jesus, it has only begun. And this is always a word that demands not only man's understanding, but also his heart. This is how it begins with Job: God intervenes in the debate, and he does not take the side of those who are defending him. He rejects as a blasphemy the apologia that makes him the cruel executioner of the pettyminded calculations of a *quid pro quo* righteousness. It is not the cries of Job that have offended God, but rather the precision of those who dare to present a terrible retributive mechanism as the face of God. And yet, nothing is explained to Job. He is only made aware of his littleness, of the poverty of the perspective from which he looks at the world. He learns to be still, to be silent, to hope. His heart is widened—and that is all. This humble act of falling silent as the first step of wisdom should concern us, too. It is a striking fact that the accusation against God hardly ever comes from the lips of those who suffer in this world. It is almost always pronounced by the well-fed onlookers, who themselves have never suffered. In this world, the hymn of God's praise ascends from the furnaces of those who suffer: the story of the three young men in the fiery furnace contains a deeper truth than all the learned treatises.[21]

The reply to Job is only a beginning, a groping anticipation of the answer that God gives with the action of his own Son in the Cross and Resurrection of Jesus Christ. Here, too, there is nothing that can be added and checked. God's answer is not an explanation but an action. The answer is a sharing in suffering—not as a mere feeling, but as reality. God's compassion has flesh. It means scourging, crowning with thorns, crucifixion, a tomb. He has

[21] I repeat here in part what I have already argued in *Dogma und Verkündigung*, pp. 331–39.

entered into our suffering. What does this mean, what can it mean? We can learn this before the great images of the crucified Jesus and the *Pietà*, where the Mother holds her dead Son. Before such images and in them, men have perceived a transformation of suffering: they have experienced that God himself dwells in the innermost sphere of their sufferings and that they became one with him precisely in their bruises. We are not speaking here of some cheap "consolation", for this experience created that love for sufferers which we see exemplified in Francis of Assisi and Elizabeth of Hungary. The crucified Christ has not removed suffering from the world. But through his Cross, he has changed men, opening their hearts to their suffering sisters and brothers and thereby strengthening and purifying them all. From him arises that "reverence for what is in our midst" which is lacking in pagan humanity and which expires where faith in the Crucified One ceases to exist. Are we not gradually beginning to grasp—thanks to all the problems connected with our "health service"—that there are some things that money cannot buy? And is not the change in contemporary society letting us gradually see something of that change which was once brought about by faith and was much more than an empty "consolation"?

We must take one further step. The Cross was not God's last word in Jesus Christ. The tomb did not hold him fast: he is risen, and God speaks to us through the Risen One. The rich glutton in hell asked that Lazarus might appear to his brothers and warn them lest they share his dreadful fate. He thinks: "If some one goes to them from the dead, they will repent" (Lk 16:27ff.). But the true Lazarus *has* come. He is here, and he speaks to us: This life is not everything. There is an eternity. Today, it is very unmodern to say this, even in theology. To speak of life beyond death looks like a flight from life here on earth. But what if it is true?

Can one simply pass it by? Can one dismiss it as mere consolation? Is it not precisely this reality that bestows on life its seriousness, its freedom, its hope?

Man is the image of God, but this image looks at us only in multiple distortions. This affirmation, in the pure sense, is true only of Jesus Christ, who is the restored image of God. But what God do we see in him? A misunderstood theology has left many people with a completely false image, the image of a cruel God who demands the blood of his own Son. They have read out of the Cross the image of Job's friends and have turned their backs on this God in horror. But the opposite is true! The biblical God demands no human sacrifices. When he appears in the course of the history of religion, human sacrifice ceases. Before Abraham can slaughter Isaac, God speaks and stops him; the ram takes the place of the child. The cult of Yahweh begins when the sacrifice of the firstborn, which was demanded by the ancestral religion of Abraham, is replaced by his obedience and his faith—the external substitute, the ram, is only the expression of this deeper reality, which is not a replacement, but rather looks ahead to the future fulfillment.[22] For the God of Israel, human sacrifice is an abomination; Moloch, the god of human sacrifices, is the embodiment of the false god who is opposed by faith in Yahweh.[23] For the God of Israel, it is, not the death of a man, but his life that is the act of worship. Irenaeus of Lyon expressed this in the wonderful formula: "Gloria Dei homo vivens" (The living man is the glorification of God).

---

[22] These brief words do not exhaust the theological depths of the sacrifice of Isaac and of its orientation to Christ. For a further elaboration, cf. L. Massignon, "Die drei Gebete Abrahams", *Internationale katholische Zeitschrift* 4 (1975): 19–28.

[23] Cf. W. Kornfeld, "Moloch", in *Bibellexikon*, ed. H. Haag, 2nd ed., pp. 1163f., with bibliography (Einsiedeln, 1968).

And this is the kind of "human sacrifice", of worship, that God demands.[24]

But in that case, what does the Lord's Cross mean? It is the form of that love which has totally accepted man and has therefore descended even into his guilt and his death. In this way, the love became a "sacrifice": as the love unbounded that takes man, the lost sheep, on its shoulders and bears him back to the Father through the night of his sin. Since then, a new form of suffering has existed: suffering, not as curse, but as a love that transforms the world.

[24] *Adversus haereses* 4, 20, 7, Sources chrétiennes 100, 648, 100.

# 2

# Jesus Christ

# Descendit de caelis—
# He came down from heaven

The section of the so-called Nicene Creed[1] that speaks of Christ begins by describing the Lord as "the Only Begotten Son of God, born of the Father before all ages. God from God, Light from Light, true God from true God, begotten, not made, consubstantial with the Father; through him all things were made." These statements in the Creed remain in the sphere that lies before the time of our world. The bridge to the earthly figure of Jesus is formed by the words: "For us men and for our salvation he came down from heaven."

The official German translation of the Missal has omitted the word *down*, doubtless because it was felt that this word presents considerable difficulties to the understanding of contemporary man. It is bound to seem offensive for two reasons. First of all, it prompts the question of whether God makes himself dependent on man. Can that which is contingent provide the reason for that which is eternal? Is it possible that the reason for God and for his action is not always God himself, and he alone?—Can God, *may* God, act in any way other than "for the sake of God"? Or

---

[1] On the history and content of the Niceno-Constantinopolitan Creed, cf. J. N. D. Kelly, *Early Christian Creeds*, 3rd ed. (London, 2006); W. Beinert, *Das Glaubensbekenntnis der Ökumene* (Freiburg i. Ue., 1973); W. Beinert, in G. Baudler, W. Beinert, and A. Kretzer, *Den Glauben bekennen* (Freiburg, 1975), pp. 34–91.

is it possible that God acts in a divine manner, for the sake of God, precisely when he acts for the sake of man?

A second offense is less profound but all the more tangible. Does not the formulation in the Creed presuppose the three-tiered image of the world that belongs to the world of myth? Does this not assume that God lives on high, above the clouds, while men live below; and that the earth is at the bottom of the creation, to which God must descend in order to restore the universe to its proper order?

In the background, even deeper questions arise, which in many ways make these first questions seem irrelevant. We do not like the idea that someone descends to another: we want, not "condescension", but rather equality. We find the words of the Magnificat, "Deposuit potentes de sede" (He has cast down the mighty from their thrones), much more to our liking than the "descendit de caelis"—although in fact the two are inseparable, since it is precisely the descending God who is the dethronement of the powerful and the raising up of those who were formerly the last, so that they now become the first. We, however, prefer to thrust down the mighty on our own, without the descending God. The image of the world in which there is no longer an "above" and a "below", the image of a world that is equal in all respects and has no fixed points of reference, is not purely external: it also corresponds to a new attitude toward reality, which regards the concept of "above" and "below" as an illusion and wants to depose every "above" for the sake of the equality, freedom, and dignity of man.

We can, however, conclude by saying that if God has descended and is now below, then the "below" has also become an "above", and the old division into "above" and "below" has been shattered. This entails a transformation in the image of the world and of man. But this change has been brought about precisely by the God who has descended.

The first thing to which we hold on is therefore this statement, which cannot be reversed or replaced by any other affirmation: he *has* descended. And this in turn means that the height, the glory, the lordship of God and of Jesus Christ *exists*; the absolute majesty of his Word, of his love, of his power *exists*. The "above"—God—exists: the second article of the Creed (which speaks of the Son) does not abolish the first (which speaks of the Father). Even in the utmost descent, even in the utmost humbling and hiddenness, God remains the true "above". Before the Creed speaks of salvation history, the fundamental confession of faith is powerfully affirmed: "God is." We must first be reminded of the inviolable majesty of the One from whom all things come, for where this is lost to sight, the descent of God, too, loses its greatness and is absorbed into the general monotony of those events that recur in aimless cycles. Where this majesty is not seen, the drama of history, the drama of human existence, loses all tension and all meaning. This does not increase man's greatness; rather, it diminishes him, since he, too, is no longer an "above" in the world, but one of its games, in which the world tries out its own possibilities. In Nietzsche's words, man becomes merely "the animal that has not yet received its definition".

Anyone who wishes to understand descent must first have grasped the mystery of the height that is indicated here by the word "heaven". The mystery of the burning bush stands at the beginning—the power that compels man to reverence and lays down the criteria he must follow. But the fire of the burning bush is not a "world fire", as Stoic philosophy understood that term: out of this fire comes forth a voice that proclaims that God has heard the groaning of the slaves, the cry of Israel's distress. This fire is itself the descent of the God who is with the lost. Accordingly, we can say that the first fruit of our reflections is that while there is no geographical descent from a higher tier of the world into a lower tier, there is something much deeper that is symbolized by the cosmic image, namely, the movement of God's being into the being of man and, even more than this, the movement out of glory into the Cross, the movement to those who are the last and who thereby become the first. Naturally, one can grasp something of the depths of what is meant by the word "descent" only when one follows the long history of this word through the writings of the Old and New Testaments, in which it begins like a little trickle and then swells into a river that unites more and more brooks and tributaries in itself. We first encounter God's "descending" in the story of the tower of Babel. This is a descent in wrath, to which a new descent out of compassion and love is then juxtaposed in the story of the burning bush. In this meditation, all I want to do is to take two representative texts, one from each Testament, which have a particular importance in the history of the motif of God's descent, although they do not in fact employ this word itself. Let us now look at them.

## 1. The beasts and the Son of Man in Daniel 7

The Book of Daniel, in the form in which we have it, is generally dated on good grounds to the years between 167 and 163 B.C., that is, the period of the harshest persecution of Israel's faith by the Hellenistic King Antiochus IV Epiphanes. In this extreme tribulation, in which the faith of the people of God, its historical hope, seems once and for all to have been reduced *ad absurdum*, the seer gains a new vision of the totality of history. After the exile, the hoped-for glory of Israel did not materialize. It remained a dependent and poor people: it failed to regain its autonomy. Instead of the magnificent new temple that Ezekiel had prophesied, it had succeeded only in building a miserable substitute that was very far from matching the splendor of the first Temple. The pilgrimage of the peoples to Israel did not take place. Instead, in its affliction, Israel itself began to be scattered among the peoples. The triumphal march of Alexander the Great and of the Hellenistic kingdoms that succeeded him put a definitive end to every hope of an improvement in Israel's situation, and skepticism was the result: Job had dared to engage in a dramatic struggle with God, but Qoheleth has nothing more to offer than a weary resignation. "All is vanity", and the only thing left is to take whatever life may have to give. Finally, the Greek Enlightenment made its victorious penetration of a somewhat empty sphere that willingly embraced the rationality of this universal culture, which was legitimated by its power and success. Only those who were open to the intellectual breadth and freedom of Greece had any chance of getting on in life now; it was obvious that history was taking the path of progress. Circumcision was regarded as an offensive pagan rite, and it disappeared; gymnasia were built and became the new centers of humanistic culture. Increasingly, the enlightened gods of Greece replaced Yahweh.

In this situation, the few believers who were left in Israel, the ludicrous minority, came to see Antiochus IV Epiphanes as the absolute symbol of those historical forces that were hostile to God; Daniel calls him a little horn (7:8) who "[speaks] great things". He is in reality a ridiculous provincial king, but the outrageous thing is that such a "little horn" is allowed to mock the God of Israel and to trample Israel's faith underfoot. But the visionary now goes on to integrate this momentary tribulation into a sequence encompassing the whole of history. This horn belongs to the fourth kingdom; world history is dominated by the sequence of four beasts that rise out of the sea. At the end, however, the earth is handed over to the one who comes from above and who is "like a son of man". The decisive point in this passage is the antithesis. The powers that up to now have ruled over the earth are beasts that come from below, out of the sea, which is the symbol of all that is dreadful, dangerous, evil. Over against them stands the man—stands Israel; the man comes from above, out of the sphere of God. For the seer, history repeats in a sense the sequence of the creation of the world, as we read this in the creation narrative. To begin with, it is the beasts that inhabit the earth, but at the end man is appointed king over the world, after God has tamed the power of chaos and ordered the sea to keep within its bounds. In the midst of the prevailing tribulation, therefore, Daniel's message is: Have no fear. The beasts may rule at present, but ultimately history will fulfill the promise of creation.[2]

Daniel's image of the Son of Man, in which the oppressed Israel expresses its hope for an end to the blasphemous power of the Hellenistic kingdoms that succeeded Alexander and portrays these as beasts that ascend from the depths, became one of the fundamental presuppositions for the profession of faith in the descent of God in Jesus Christ, the Son of Man. It is a part of the background that gives meaning to this affirmation in our Creed. In this perspective, it tells us that the foe of that which comes from below,

---

[2] On this, cf. N. W. Porteous, *Das Buch Daniel*, 2nd ed., ATD 3 (Göttingen, 1968), pp. 74–96, esp. 79f.

of the bestial power that destroys the world in its arrogant brutality, is the "man" who comes from above. And this antithesis includes both his powerlessness and his victory. He is powerless, because man is not an animal. He does not possess the greedy mouth, the teeth of iron, the claws of brass, and the horns that make such a terrible din—before weapons of this kind, he cannot defend himself and is lost. But this same image expresses his victory, too. At the end, it is the man who is the king of the beasts, and he will subdue them with a different power, the hidden power of the spirit and of the heart that has been bestowed on him. At the end, the power belongs to him: and this means at the same time that "power" is transformed.

Jesus, the Son of God, comes among the beasts as a man. In the weakness of a man, he establishes the sovereignty of God. Precisely through the sign of the weakness that takes its stand against brutality, he embodies the sovereignty of God. He comes among the beasts without himself becoming an animal, without adopting their methods. And he is devoured. But this is precisely how he conquers them. The defeat that he accepts is the victory of that which is different: there exists something other than the bestial. There is "love to the end" (see Jn 13:1). And this brings about the restoration of man.

He goes among the beasts in the form of man. And this means that he seeks those who are with him, those who take his side, those who trust the power of the "man from above" and thus allow him to redeem them.

## 2. Descent as a spiritual event

The tenth chapter of the Letter to the Hebrews contains one of the most profound interpretations of the descent of the Son. Here every spatial idea has disappeared, so that the personal and spiritual substance of this way of reflecting on Christ shines out in full splendor. The author of the epistle begins by repeating once again his basic idea that animal sacrifices are not suited to restore the right relationship between man and God. He then continues: "Consequently, when Christ came into the world, he said, 'Sacrifices and offerings you have not desired, but a body have you prepared for me; in burnt offerings and sin offerings you have taken no pleasure. Then I said, "Behold, I have come to do your will, O God," as it is written of me in the roll of the book'" (Heb 10:5–7). With the help of a quotation from Psalm 40 [39]:6–8, which is interpreted here as the prayer spoken by Jesus when he came into the world, the Letter offers a genuine theology of the Incarnation, in which there is no trace of cosmic tiers. Rather, the "descending" and "entering" are understood here as an act of prayer; and certainly, prayer is conceived here as a genuine act, as laying claim to the totality of existence, which, in prayer, starts to move and gives itself away. Christ's entry into the cosmos is understood here as a voluntary and verbal event, as the concrete realization of the kind of thinking and believing that emerges in the piety of so many psalms.

Let us now look more closely at the text of the psalm and its transformation in the New Testament. What does this psalm say? It is the thanksgiving made by one whom God has raised from the dead.[3] His understanding of true

---

[3] In the Old Testament text, this refers to "the sphere of death", the "realm of the dead": H.-J. Kraus, *Psalmen* I (Neukirchen, 1960), pp. 305–10 (at p. 307). It is only in the New Testament that the text acquires its full realism thanks to its relationship to the real death and the real Resurrection of Christ. Through its transposition in Hebrews 10 back behind the Incarnation into the dialogue within the Godhead, the affirmation takes on yet another new dimension.

piety does not lead the man who utters this prayer to offer an animal in sacrifice. In keeping with the prophetic tradition, he is aware that: "Sacrifice and offering you do not desire; but you have given me an open ear" (Ps 40 [39]:6). In other words, God wants, not things, but the ears of man, his hearing, his obedience, and therein man himself. Man's true thanksgiving, the thanksgiving that is in accordance with God, means entering into the will of God.

The Letter to the Hebrews sees these words from the psalm as the revelation of that dialogue between the Father and the Son which is the Incarnation. The author thus recognizes the Incarnation as an event within the Trinity, as a spiritual event. In the light of the fulfillment in Jesus, he has changed only one word in the text. Instead of the "ear", the sense of hearing, Hebrews speaks of the body: "A body have you prepared for me." This "body" is human existence itself, the sharing in the *natura humana*. Obedience becomes incarnate. In its highest fulfillment, it is no longer a mere act of hearing: it becomes flesh. The theology of the Word becomes the theology of the Incarnation. The Son's gift of himself to the Father emerges from the dialogue within the Godhead; it becomes the acceptance, and thus the gift, of that creation which finds its synthesis in man. This body, or more correctly the humanity of Jesus, is the product of obedience, the fruit of the loving response of the Son; it is, so to speak, prayer that has taken on a concrete form. In this sense, Jesus' humanity is something wholly spiritual, something that is "divine" because of its origin.

If we reflect on this, we see that the humbling involved in the Incarnation and, indeed, the descent involved in the Cross correspond on a profound level to the very mystery of the Son. Essentially, the Son is the release and handing back of himself—that is what sonship means. When the

Son is translated into the creation, it means "[obedience] unto death, even death on a cross" (Phil 2:8). The text of Hebrews addresses us very directly out of the sublimity of the mystery. We do not become God by making ourselves independent or by attempting to live in the unbounded autonomy of one who is fully emancipated. Such attempts break down because of their inherent contradictions, because they are ultimately untrue. We become God by sharing in the gesture of the Son. We become God by becoming "child", "son"; we become God when we enter into the words that Jesus addresses to the Father and when our dialogue with the Father enters into the flesh of our daily life: "A body have you prepared for me...."

Our salvation means becoming "the body of Christ", becoming like Christ himself, receiving ourselves from him every day and giving ourselves back every day, offering our body every day as the place where the Word can dwell. We become like Christ by following him, descending and ascending. All this is expressed by the simple words *descendit de caelis*—words that speak of Christ and, thereby, speak of us. This profession of faith is not exhausted by the act of speaking: it points us from the word to the body. It is only in the movement from the word to the body and from the body to the word that we can truly make it our own.

# *". . . and became man"*

The affirmation about the Incarnation of God is the central proposition of the Christian Creed. The theologians in every century have reflected on this, attempting to understand in its light something of the mystery of God and of man. These great questions penetrate the depths, and we shall not present them here. All I wish to do is to look for a little theological lane, so that we can learn to grasp that which is great and far away on the basis of that which is near at hand and simple, something that touches our own lives. We will be guided here by the following consideration. One can consider human existence in terms of its basic components, such as spirit and body, Creator and creation, the individual and the community, or history as the sphere in which we live. But one can also go beyond these great and comprehensive structures that give the individual his place in the totality and reflect on the fact that the individual never possesses his life in its completeness in one single moment; even in the individual, life has a temporal extension, and it is only the totality of this temporal structure that makes him the man he is. In this temporal dimension of the individual man, the specifically human link between biology and spirit is at work: man's time is characterized by the biological sequence of childhood, maturity, old age, and death, and it is in these biological phases that his life unfolds. The piety of the Middle Ages and the early modern period liked to dwell on this aspect when it meditated on the humanity of Jesus; it spoke of the "mysteries of

the life of Jesus", referring to the individual phases of
Jesus' earthly, historical path.[4] This contemplative prayer,
which then gave rise to meditative paintings, pondered
lovingly the earthly seasons of Jesus' life in order to experience therein, at very close quarters, the immeasurable
reality that we profess when we say that "the Son of God
became man." Surely it is not completely impossible to
attempt to do something similar today? Let us take a few
first steps along this path—more is not possible—and
reflect on what it means to say that Jesus lived his humanity in the sequence of childhood, adulthood, and death.

## 1. The childhood of Jesus

He became a child. What does it mean to be a child?[5]
To begin with, it means dependence, needing support and
help from others. As a child, Jesus came not only from
God, but from other human beings. He grew in the womb
of a woman, from whom he received his flesh and his
blood, his heartbeat, his gestures, his language. He received
life from the life of another human being. This derivation
from others of that which is his own is not a merely biological reality. It means that Jesus also received the forms
of thinking and of looking at things, all that was imprinted
upon his human soul, from the men before him and, in
the last analysis, from his mother. It means that when he
received the inheritance of his ancestors, he accepted in

[4] For a good historical overview, cf. A. Grillmeier, *Mit ihm und in ihm: Chris-
tologische Forschungen und Perspektiven* (Freiburg, 1975), pp. 716–36.

[5] We can only touch on this question in a meditative manner here; we can-
not examine it in greater philosophical depth. See the penetrating analysis by
F. Ulrich, *Der Mensch als Anfang: Zur philosophischen Anthropologie der Kindheit*
(Einsiedeln, 1970).

himself the whole winding path that leads back from Mary to Abraham and ultimately back to Adam. He bore within himself the burden of this history; he transformed it by his own life and suffering, bringing it out of all the denials and the upsets to God's plan into the pure Yes: "For the Son of God, Jesus Christ, ... was not Yes and No; but in him it is always Yes" (2 Cor 1:19).

It is striking to note that Jesus himself finds it so important for human existence that we be children: "Truly, I say to you, unless you turn and become like children, you will never enter the kingdom of heaven" (Mt 18:3). This means that Jesus does not regard "being a child" as a transient phase of human life that is a consequence of man's biological fate and then is completely laid aside. Rather, it is in "being a child" that the very essence of what it is to be a man is realized, so much so that one who has lost the essence of childhood is himself lost. We could then reflect, in a spirit of human empathy, that if being a child remained so precious in Jesus' eyes and he saw this as the purest mode of human existence, then he must have had very happy memories of his own childhood days; and this could teach us reverence vis-à-vis children, who appeal to our love precisely in their defenselessness. Above all, however, we must ask: What is the true nature of this childhood that Jesus considers so irreplaceable? For it is clear that Jesus is not indulging in a romantic glorification of childhood. Nor is he pronouncing a moral judgment. Something deeper is involved here.

The first point that we must ponder is the fact that the central name that designates the dignity of Jesus is "the Son". Irrespective of how we may wish to answer the question of whether this term was anticipated *linguistically* in the way Jesus spoke of himself, there can be no doubt that this term tries to summarize in a single word the total impression that his life made. The orientation of his life, the root from which it sprang, and the goal that marked it—all this bears the name *Abba*, "dear Father". Jesus knew that he was never alone. His whole existence until his final cry on the Cross was one single act of reaching out to that Other whom he called "Father". This is the only possible explanation of the historical fact that when a name was sought that expressed Jesus' dignity, no attribute such as "king" or "lord" won the day, but rather a noun that could also be translated as "child". We are therefore entitled to affirm that if Jesus' own preaching so strongly emphasizes "being a child", this is because of the profound correspondence between this and his own most personal mystery, namely, his sonship. His highest dignity, which points to his divinity, is ultimately no power that he possesses on his own: it is rooted in the fact that his existence is oriented to the Other, namely, to God the Father.

Joachim Jeremias once made the very beautiful observation that being a child, as Jesus understands this, means learning to say "Father".[6] If we are to grasp the full weight of this word "Father", however, we must remember how Jesus understands his own sonship: for here we meet once again all that we pondered in our first meditations on the triune God and on the Creator God. Man wishes to be God, and this is indeed his destiny. But where he attempts to achieve this goal, as in the ever-recurring conversation with the serpent in paradise, by emancipating himself from God and his creation, taking an autonomous stance and trusting in his own powers, or, in other words, where he becomes completely grown-up and completely

---

[6] J. Jeremias, *Neutestamentliche Theologie*, vol. 1, *Die Verkündigung Jesu* (Gütersloh, 1971), p. 154: "To become a child once more" means learning once more to say "Abba".

emancipated and completely rejects the mode of existence that is designated by "being a child", he ends up in utter emptiness, because he stands in contradiction to his own truth, which means a relatedness. It is only if he preserves the innermost core of "being a child", the existence as son that Jesus exemplifies for us, that he enters with the Son into "being God".

This is of course an extremely general remark. Another aspect of what Jesus means by "being a child" becomes visible in his praise of the poor: "Blessed are you poor, for yours is the kingdom of God" (Lk 6:20). In this beatitude, the poor have replaced the children. This is no romantic exaltation of poverty, nor is Jesus uttering moral judgments about individual rich and poor people. Rather, what is concerned here is the very depth of what it is to be human. "Being poor" lets us see something of what "being a child" means: a child possesses nothing of his own. He lives from others, and he is free precisely in the fact that he has neither power nor possessions. He does not yet occupy any position that masks and crushes his own true character. Possessions and power are the two great temptations faced by man, who becomes the prisoner of his own goods and throws away his own soul for the sake of these goods. Anyone who cannot remain a poor man even in the midst of his possessions—a poor man who knows that the world is in God's hands, not his own—has lost that "being a child" without which there is no access to the kingdom. In this context, Stylianos Harkianakis has pointed out that in the dialogue *Timaeus*, Plato speaks of the ironic judgment of a non-Greek who notes that the Greeks are *aei paides*, "eternal children". Plato sees this, not as a reproach, but as praise of the Greek character. "At any rate, it is clear that the Greeks wanted to be a people of philosophers, not of technocrats, eternal children who

regarded astonishment as the highest state of human existence. Only so can we explain the significant fact that the
Greeks did not put their innumerable inventions to any
practical use."[7]

Here, too, in this allusion to the tacit relationship between the Greek soul and the message of the Gospel, we
find a message for ourselves: the astonishment in man must
not wither away, this capacity for astonishment and for listening that does not merely inquire into the usefulness of
things, but hears the harmony of the spheres and rejoices
precisely at that which does not serve the practical pur-
poses of man.

There is one further step that we must take. We have
seen that "being a child" means saying "Father", and
we must now add: "being a child" also means saying
"Mother". If we eliminate this, we eliminate the human
dimension of Jesus' "being a child". All that remains is the
sonship of the Logos, although it is precisely the human
child Jesus who is meant to reveal this sonship to us. This
idea has been expressed so marvelously by Hans Urs von
Balthasar that it is worth quoting his words at length:

> *Eucharistia* means thanksgiving. How wonderful that Jesus
> gives thanks by endlessly offering himself and making a
> gift of himself to God and to men! Whom does he thank?
> Most certainly, he thanks God the Father, the model and
> ultimate source of all giving.... But he surely also thanks
> the poor sinners who are willing to receive him, who
> let him enter under their unworthy roof. Is there any-
> one else whom he thanks? I would say that he thanks the
> poor Maid from whom he received this flesh and blood

---

[7] S. Harkianakis, *Orthodoxe Kirche und Katholizismus* (Munich, 1975), pp. 6of.
I myself believe that the passage in Plato (the conversation between an Egyptian
priest and Solon, *Timaeus* 22b) has a somewhat different accentuation in the
original text, but we need not discuss this question here.

through the overshadowing of the Holy Spirit.... What does Jesus learn from his mother? He learns to say Yes, *fiat*. Not just any Yes, but a Yes that goes ever farther, without getting weary. Everything that you desire, my God.... "Behold, I am the handmaid of the Lord, let it be done to me according to your word." ... This is the Catholic prayer that Jesus learned from his human mother, from the *Catholica Mater* who was in the world before him and who was inspired by God to be the first to speak this word of the new and eternal covenant.[8]

In the essay by Stylianos Harkianakis, we find a comment in which the logic of the child has taken on a form so pure and convincing that, in comparison, all rational justifications are merely pale abstractions devoid of the brilliance of the child's way of seeing things:

A monk from the monastery of Iviron once told me: "We revere the Mother of God and have placed all our hope in her, since we know that she can do all things. And do you know why she can do all things? Her Son leaves no wish of hers unfulfilled, because he has not returned that which he borrowed from her. He borrowed flesh from her; he did indeed deify this flesh, but he did not give it back to her. This is the reason why we feel so safe in the garden of the Mother of God!"[9]

## 2. Nazareth

Nazareth has been distorted for us by the painters of the "Nazarene" school. The name of this town in large part stands for a mawkish transformation of the life of Jesus

[8] Hans Urs von Balthasar, "Haus des Gebetes", in W. Seidel, *Kirche aus lebendigen Steinen* (Mainz, 1975), pp. 11–29, at 25ff.

[9] Harkianakis, *Orthodoxe Kirche*, p. 65.

into a petit-bourgeois idyll that we dismiss as a belittlement of the mystery. The origin of our veneration of the Holy Family, which often falls under this verdict, was in fact completely different. This devotion was initiated by Cardinal Laval in Canada in the eighteenth century as an appeal to the laity to assume their own proper responsibility. The Cardinal "recognized at that time the need to give the colonial population a solid societal structure, to prevent them from sinking into degeneration through their lack of roots and traditions. He did not have enough priests to form compact eucharistic communities.... So he dedicated his entire attention to the family: the life of prayer was entrusted to the father of the family."[10] On the basis of Nazareth, the house and the family were discovered as a church, and the father of the household was urged to assume his priestly responsibility. In "Galilee of the Gentiles", Jesus grew up as a Jew. Without attending a school, he acquired his knowledge of the Scriptures in the house in which the Word of God had its dwelling.[11] The hints in Luke may be brief, but they suffice to give us an idea of the spirit of responsibility and openness, of the piety and the honesty that marked this community and made it a realization of the true Israel. Above all, however, the subsequent activity of Jesus, who read the Scriptures and knew them with the certainty of a teacher, just as he knew the traditions of the rabbis, shows how fruitful his learning had been in the life he shared in Nazareth. And

[10] T. Maertens and J. Frisque, *Kommentar zum Messbuch* I (Freising, 1965), p. 166.

[11] On the period of Jesus' youth, see the impressive account, based on archaeological discoveries, by B. Schwank, "Das Theater von Sepphoris und die Jugendjahre Jesu", *Erbe und Auftrag* 52 (1976): 199–206. This article contains valuable correctives both to the usual picture of the Judaism of Jesus' days and to recent Jewish scholarship about Jesus. R. Aron, *Die verborgenen Jahre Jesu* (Frankfurt, 1962), is also worth reading.

does all this say nothing to us, in an age in which most Christians are obliged to live in a "Galilee of the Gentiles"? The universal Church can grow and flourish only if she is aware that her hidden roots are kept safe in the atmosphere of Nazareth.

Another perspective is just as important. Although the contemporaries noticed nothing, the true mystery of Nazareth was rediscovered in its deepest form, right in the midst of all the "Nazarene kitsch", by Charles de Foucauld, who found Nazareth when he searched for "the lowest place". On his pilgrimage to the Holy Land, it was this town that most affected him: he did not feel called "to follow Jesus in public life, but Nazareth touched him in the depths of his heart."[12] He wanted to follow the silent Jesus, the poor man, the worker. He wanted to obey literally the words of Jesus: "When you are invited, go and sit in the lowest place" (Lk 14:10). He knew that Jesus himself was the first to expound these words by showing in his life what they meant. He knew that even before Jesus died on the Cross, naked and without any possessions at all, he had chosen the lowest place in Nazareth. Charles de Foucauld found his Nazareth first in the Trappist monastery of Notre-Dame des Neiges in 1890, but he found it again only six months later in the even poorer community of Syrian Trappist nuns, Notre-Dame du Sacré-Coeur. From there, he wrote to his sister: "We do farm laborers' work, work that is infinitely wholesome for the soul, work during which one can pray and meditate.... You really understand what a piece of bread is when you know from your own experience how much hard work it takes to produce it."[13]

[12] M. Carrouges, *Charles de Foucauld: Forscher und Beter* (Freiburg, 1958), p. 120.

[13] Ibid., p. 134.

As he followed the tracks of the "mysteries of Jesus' life", Charles de Foucauld discovered Jesus the worker. He met the genuine "historical Jesus". In 1892, while Charles de Foucauld was working in Notre-Dame du Sacré-Coeur, Martin Kähler's epoch-making book *Der sogenannte historische Jesus und der geschichtliche, biblische Christus* (The socalled historical Jesus and the historic, biblical Christ) was published in Europe. This was one of the first high points in the controversy about the historical Jesus. The brother in the Syrian convent knew nothing about this, but when he entered into Jesus' Nazareth experience, he came to understand more about the historical Jesus than scholarly discussion can ever bring to light. There, in living meditation on Jesus, a new way opened up for the Church. For working alongside Jesus the worker, the immersion in "Nazareth", became the starting point for the idea and the praxis of the worker priest. It became a rediscovery of poverty for the Church. Nazareth has an abiding message for the Church. The New Covenant begins, not in the Temple or on the holy mountain, but in the simple dwelling of the Virgin, in the house of the worker, in one of the forgotten places in "Galilee of the Gentiles", a town from which no one expected anything good to come. The Church can always begin anew from that place and recover her health from that place. If the Church is to make the correct response to our century's cries of protest against the power of riches, Nazareth must remain an experiential reality in her own self.

### 3. Public activity and hiddenness

The period of silence, of learning, and of waiting is followed by work: Jesus emerges into public activity. Jesus' humanity also means sharing in the joy and the success that public activity can bring, sharing in the happiness of human work that is brought to a successful conclusion. Naturally, it also means sharing in the burden and in the risk that are linked to public activity. One who works in public does not only gain friends; he also exposes himself to contradiction, misunderstanding, and abuse. His name and his Word can now be twisted to the right and to the left by the various parties. The Antichrist dons the mask of Christ, and he will use this as the devil uses the Word of God, the Bible (Mt 4:1–11; Lk 4:1–13). And paradoxically, public activity always entails isolation. This is what happens to Jesus, too: he gathers friends around him, but he is not spared either the disappointment of a friendship that is betrayed or the lack of understanding on the part of his well-meaning but weak disciples. At the end comes the lonely hour of fear on the Mount of Olives, when the disciples sleep: in his innermost core, he remains misunderstood.

In addition to this loneliness of being misunderstood, there is another way in which Jesus is solitary and alone. He has lived his life on the basis of a point that others could not reach, namely, on the basis of his being alone with God. The words of William of Saint-Thierry apply to him completely and more profoundly than they can ever apply to any other man: "He who is with God is never less alone than when he is alone."[14] Of the four evangelists, it is Luke who treats this subject in the most penetrating manner, and I should therefore like to analyze briefly three significant passages in his Gospel; but we begin by looking at a passage in Mark that shows that on this precise point, Luke, even if he has special emphases of his own, stands within the tradition shared by all the evangelists.

[14] Quotation in ibid., p. 168.

Let us therefore begin with Mark (6:45–52; cf. Mt 14:22–33), who relates that after the multiplication of the loaves, Jesus withdraws alone to "the" mountain, in order to pray. The disciples set out on the lake. He is alone on land, while they struggle on the water but make no progress, because the wind is against them. Jesus prays, and in his prayer he *sees* how they make headway painfully, so he comes to them. It is clear that this text is full of ecclesiological symbolism: the disciples facing strong headwinds on the sea, the Lord with the Father. But the decisive point is this: in his prayer, when he is with the Father, he is not absent from them. In his prayer, he *sees* them. Where Jesus is with the Father, the Church too is present. Here, the problem of the Second Coming of the Lord is taken onto a deeper, trinitarian level and transformed: Jesus sees the Church in the Father, and on the basis of the Father's might, in the power drawn from his speaking with the Father, he is present to the Church. It is precisely his speaking with the Father, his being on the mountain, that makes him present, and so we can say that the Church is, as it were, the object of the conversation between the Father and the Son and is thereby anchored in theology.

The first text in Luke that I wish to present is the calling of the Twelve (Lk 6:12–16). According to Luke, their vocation is the fruit of a night that Jesus spends in prayer (we may recall the beautiful words of Saint Ambrose: "Jesus spent a whole night awake in prayer for you, and what do you do for your salvation?"). The difference between this narrative and the account of the same event in Matthew is particularly illuminating. In Matthew, the calling of the Twelve follows Jesus' exhortation to "pray ... the Lord of the harvest to send out laborers into his harvest" (9:38). The choice of the Twelve appears as the first answer to this prayer. It is as though Jesus himself were anticipating the response that the divine authority would subsequently make to the prayer of his disciples. In Luke, the act of calling the Twelve is located in the nocturnal prayer of the Lord on the mountain. The apostolate has its theological *locus* (in the strict sense of this term) in his solitary dialogue with the Father. To put it differently: here we are permitted to see that the apostolate has a theological *locus*, that it is the fruit of the dialogue between the Son's will and the Father's will, and that it will always be sheltered and kept safe within this dialogue.

The second text is Luke's version of the story of the Transfiguration (9:28–36). According to Luke, this takes place while Jesus prays: "And as he was praying, the appearance of his countenance was altered." In his prayer, the innermost essence of the mystery of Jesus becomes visible, and we see who he really is. Some scholars have alleged that this is a Resurrection narrative that has been transposed back into the earthly life of Jesus, but perhaps it would be more correct to speak of a "Resurrection appearance". It is possible for the Father to permit an appearance in the glory that radiates forth from himself even before the Resurrection, since the inner foundation of the Resurrection is already present in the earthly Jesus, that is, the immersion of the core of his existence in his dialogue with the Father, an immersion that is also the glory of the Son and is, indeed, the very form his sonship takes. His Passion and death would then mean that his entire earthly existence, too, is poured out into the total dialogue of love, where the fire of love transforms it.

This allows us to affirm that Luke has raised the prayer of Jesus to the central christological category from which he describes the mystery of the Son. What Chalcedon expressed by means of a formula drawn from the sphere of Greek ontology is affirmed by Luke in an utterly personal category based on the historical experience of the earthly Jesus; in substantial terms, this corresponds completely to the formula of Chalcedon. This is confirmed in a third text, the central profession of faith in Christ that Matthew localizes in Caesarea Philippi and links to the promise that Peter will receive the primacy. At Luke 9:18, this profession of faith proceeds from Jesus' praying and is a response to it. It is, so to speak, the synthesis of what happens in Jesus' prayer. "Now it happened that as he was praying alone the disciples were with him, and he asked them, 'Who do the people say that I am?'" The paradox in this passage is obvious. While he was *alone*, the disciples were with him: the deliberate contradiction makes it clear that Luke is not simply relating a chain of historical happenings; rather, he is writing theology. Those who do not know the solitude of Jesus take him to be this or that; but the profession of faith translates into human language what Jesus really is, since it sees what truly "drives" him, namely, his solitary speaking with the Father. If the profession of faith is to grow, it must share in Jesus' solitude, in being with him where he is alone with the Father.

The public activity of Jesus has its center in this hiddenness, in which it embraces the public dimension of the whole world. It is from this hiddenness that he comes to men and that he is with them; and it is in this hiddenness that men gain access to him.

## 4. Death and Resurrection

To be human means to make one's way toward death. To be human means that one must die. It means being a thing of contradictions: on the one hand, biology decrees that dying is natural and necessary, but, on the other hand, a center of the spirit has opened up in man's *bios*, a center that demands eternity, and this makes dying not natural but illogical, an expulsion from the realm of love, the destruction of a communication that of its essence tends toward permanence.

In this world, living means dying. Hence, "he became man" also means that he made his way toward death. In him, the contradictoriness inherent in man's death becomes utterly acute, since in Jesus, whose whole existence is in the shared dimension of his dialogue with the Father, the absolute solitude wrought by death is simply incomprehensible. On the other hand, in him, too, death has a necessity all its own. For we have seen that his existence with the Father is the reason why he is misunderstood by men and is alone in the midst of his public activity. His execution is the final, consistent act of this failure to understand, of this expulsion of the one who is misunderstood into the zone of silence.

This may perhaps help us to sense something of the inner, theological dimension of his death, since in the case of men, dying is always both a biological event and an event involving the human spirit. Here, the destruction of the bodily instrument of communication interrupts his dialogue with the Father. When the bodily instrument is crushed, the intellectual act that is based on this instrument disappears for a time. And this means that more is shattered here than in any other human death: here, that dialogue which in truth is the axis of the whole world is broken off. Jesus' dying cry from Psalm 22 [21]—"My God, my God, why have you forsaken me?"—shows us something of the mysterious depths of this event. But just as this dialogue isolates Jesus and is the reason for both the fact of his death and its terrible enormity, so too this dialogue contains in itself the reason for his Resurrection: for it is through the

Resurrection that his human existence is brought into the trinitarian dialogue of eternal love itself. His human existence can never perish again; beyond the threshold of death, it rises up anew and takes on its fullness anew.

Thus, it is only the Resurrection that discloses the final, decisive point in the article of the Creed: "He ... became man." The Resurrection teaches us something that now possesses eternal validity: he *is* man. He remains man forever. Through him, human existence has been admitted into God's own being: this is the fruit of his death. We are *in* God. God is both the one who is utterly "other" and the one who is "not other".[15] When we say "Father" with Jesus, we say it in God himself. This is the hope of man, the Christian joy, the Good News: even today, he is man. In him, God has truly become the one who is "not other". Man, that absurd being, is no longer absurd. Man, that comfortless being, is no longer comfortless: we are allowed to rejoice. He loves us! God loves us in such a way that his Word became flesh and remains flesh. This joy ought to be the strongest impulse and the strongest force in us, leading us to communicate it to others so that they, too, may rejoice in the light that has dawned for us and proclaims the day to the world in the middle of the night.

[15] On this, cf. Hans Urs von Balthasar, "Evangelium und Philosophie", *Freiburger Zeitschrift für Philosophie und Theologie* 23 (1976): 3–12.

# Consubstantial with the Father

In 1975, the anniversary of the first ecumenical council, the Council of Nicaea (325), was celebrated in many places. This council made the divinity of Jesus the inalienable possession of the Church's faith by inserting one single philosophical term into the Creed: *homoousios*, "consubstantial with the Father". And this is why remembering that council is directly relevant to the renewed controversy about Christology that confronts us today. We see this in questions that might at first sight seem to show that Nicaea is hopelessly out of date—questions such as the following: Can words from so remote a past still mean anything for us today? Can their problems still concern us and their answers still help us? Is there any use in celebrating the past? Is it not much more necessary to equip ourselves to face the present and the future? If one looks more closely at the council, his suspicions will only be strengthened: this council defined the divine sonship of Jesus, but is it not precisely this divine sonship that removes us far from Jesus and makes him inaccessible to us? Is it not the man Jesus whom we can understand even today and who even today can make people uneasy? Is it not time to turn our backs on the golden splendor of the divinity and get passionate about the man Jesus, discovering here that passion for the humanity of man that is so appropriate to this hour in history? The main word of the council is *homoousios*—Jesus is consubstantial with the Father. Does this not merely confirm our suspicions? Does it not mean that the faith has been turned into a matter of philosophy?

That may perhaps have been inevitable in the fourth century, but what does that have to do with us today? Was not faith surrendered to the Greek search for the "essence"? And would it not be both biblical and modern to abandon this question about the "essence" of Jesus and get involved with history, since we cannot shirk the task of responding to history's challenging appeal?

If one refuses to remain on the superficial level, one will quickly hear the answering objections: All that was written in the previous paragraph may indeed seem obvious, but is it not perhaps ultimately a flight from the true greatness that we encounter here? After the Council of Chalcedon (451), Emperor Leo I asked the bishops what they thought of the decisions taken by this assembly. Thirty-four replies, bearing the signatures of about 280 bishops or monks, have survived in the so-called Codex Encyclius. One of the bishops whose words are recorded sums up the spirit of the entire document when he says that the bishops sought to answer "piscatorie et non Aristotelice", like fishermen, not like philosophers.[16] These words could just as well have been said by one of the conciliar fathers at Nicaea, since they perfectly describe the attitude that inspired the bishops in their fight against the temptations of Arianism. They were not interested in the questions of scholars, twisting around in an ever more refined subtlety. They were interested in the simple point that got lost to view behind such questions: they were interested in the simple basic questions of simple people. The panorama of academic reflection is in continual flux, but these basic questions have an enduring character, since the fundamental structure of human relatedness, the simple center of

---

[16] For a detailed study of the Codex Encyclius and its theological contents, cf. A. Grillmeier, *Mit ihm und in ihm*, pp. 283–300.

man's existence, is always the same. The nearer our questions come to this center, the more they lie in the very heart of what it is to be a man, and the simpler they are, the less it is possible to declare them obsolete.

"Piscatorie, non Aristotelice": Must we not then ask who this Jesus really was? Is it irrelevant to us whether he was a man or more than that? Surely this question is irrelevant only if we have dismissed the second alternative a priori as an impossibility. But if he was really only a man like any of us, what was happening then, and what happens now? Can one expect that an enthusiasm for a Jesus of that kind will last? Is our enthusiasm for Jesus not due to the splendor of the faith that has attributed importance to him down through the centuries? And is this enthusiasm not doomed to a speedy demise where this splendor disappears? Where all that is left is the man Jesus, men themselves will not long endure. Karl Jaspers, with the sympathy felt by a philosopher who comes from the Christian tradition, has attempted to retain the importance of Jesus by seeing him as the definitive man; but what remains is in reality only an exceptional existence that cannot offer any direct guidance for the lives of other men. What remains is empty and ultimately has nothing to say to us. This applies to every form of veneration based on the man Jesus alone: where all that is left is the man, men themselves cannot remain.

That which makes Jesus important and irreplaceable in every age is precisely the fact that he was and is the Son, that in him God has become man. The God does not suppress the man: on the contrary, it is the God who makes the man precious and infinitely important. To remove the God from Jesus does not mean discovering the man Jesus. It means obliterating the man Jesus for the sake of self-made ideals of short duration.

"Who was Jesus?" is a "fisherman's question", not a problem of a philosophical ontology alien to us today. No change could ever supersede this question or deprive it of its importance. It is only if Jesus was God, only if God became man in him, that something actually took place in him. It is only then that the melancholy skepticism in Qoheleth's words is shattered: "There is nothing new under the sun." It is only then that something has happened, only then that history has truly occurred, if it is indeed true that Jesus *is* the Son of God. Precisely this *Being* is the tremendous *event* on which everything depends.

But why did Arius' answer seem so very obvious to the people of his age? Why did he succeed in winning over the public opinion of the entire educated world in so short a time? His success was due to the same reason that leads public opinion today to write off the Council of Nicaea: Arius wanted to preserve the purity of the concept of God. He did not want to ascribe to God anything as naïve as an incarnation. He was convinced that, in the final analysis, the concept of God and God himself must be completely excluded from human history. He was convinced that, ultimately, the world itself must regulate its own affairs; that it cannot gain access to God; and that of course God himself is so great that he cannot touch the world. The Fathers regarded this as atheism, and their judgment was correct, since a God to whom man has no access whatsoever, a God who in reality cannot play any role in the world, is no God. But have we not long since quietly returned to this kind of atheism? Do we, too, not find it intolerable to make God descend into human existence? Do we, too, not find it impossible that man could have a genuine relationship with God in the world? Is this not the reason why we have retreated with such passion to "the man Jesus"? But does this not mean that we have

ended up in a world view of despair? For if only we ourselves have power over the world, since God has no such
power, what else remains but despair (even if it is screened
by big words)?

"Piscatorie, non Aristotelice"—well, we might say, it is
indeed true that the Fathers of Nicaea posed their questions
like fishermen, not like philosophers. And this means that
the questions they posed were our questions, the deepest
and most insuperable questions. But did they also *answer*
like fishermen? Was not their answer philosophical? Is the
*homoousios* a fisherman's answer? Does it not rather belong
to Aristotle and, hence, to the past? Everything seems to
plead in favor of this judgment. But let us look at what is
actually involved here.

In the process of the formation of the Creed, one of the
many names with which the faith in the beginning had
encircled the mystery of Jesus gradually emerged as the
center that encompassed everything else: the word "Son".
This word is rooted in Jesus' own act of praying, and it
points to his innermost dimension. From the perspective
of human thinking, however, it remains a *metaphor* when
we apply it to God. How far, then, does this metaphor go?
How literally may or must it be taken? The entire world
will be different, my life and the life of all of us will be
different, depending on whether this is religious poetry or
an affirmation of the uttermost seriousness. The Fathers of
Nicaea intended the little word *homoousios* to be the simple
translation of the metaphor "Son" into a concept. Their
word affirms something very simple, namely, that "Son"
is not a mere comparison, but literal reality. In its very
heart, in the testimony it bears to Jesus Christ, the Bible
must be taken literally. The Word is literally true—*that* is
what is meant by calling Jesus "consubstantial" with the
Father. This is not placing philosophy on an equal footing

with the Bible; on the contrary, it protects the Bible from attack by philosophy. In the hermeneutical debates, it protects the literal meaning of Scripture. What the Fathers actually said here is a "fisherman's" answer: the Word is to be taken at its word. It is true as written. This is the audacious greatness of the conciliar affirmation, which is no mere human achievement, the elaboration of a wonderful concept: it opens the path out of the conceptual debates back into the living center of the Word. The Word is true in its simplicity, and precisely *this* is its exciting greatness. It is not a thought, but reality. The Son is truly the Son. The martyrs died for this truth, and Christians of all ages live on the basis of this truth. Only a reality of this kind can endure.[17]

But what gives the Church the courage to make such a profession of faith? And who or what can show us the way to such a profession? Let us conclude these reflections by listening to the Lord himself and to the answer he gives: "I thank you, Father, Lord of heaven and earth, that you have hidden these things from the wise and understanding and revealed them to infants; yes, Father, for such was your gracious will. All things have been delivered to me by my Father; and no one knows the Son except the Father, and no one knows the Father except the Son and any one to whom the Son chooses to reveal him" (Mt 11:25–27). What does this mean? First of all, it says something very simple and clear: God can be known only through God. No one other than God himself can know God. This act of knowing, in which God knows himself, is God's giving of himself as Father and God's receiving of himself

---

[17] On this, cf. the International Theological Commission, *Die Einheit des Glaubens und der theologische Pluralismus* (Einsiedeln, 1973), pp. 61–67, especially 65ff.

and giving back of himself as Son, the exchange of eternal love, both the eternal gift and the eternal return of this gift. Since this is so, it is also possible for "anyone to whom the Son chooses to reveal him" to know God. This will of the Son is not arbitrary, like the will of the tyrants and the powerful men of this world. The will of the Son embraces the one who voluntarily accepts to be in it; the will of the Son embraces the one who himself lives like a son, through the mercy of God—one who has not cast off the mystery of "being a child"—one who is not so adult, so well established in life, that it would be impossible for him to say "Father", to know that he owes his existence to God and to give himself back to God. This is why there is a secret correspondence between immaturity and knowledge: not because Christianity is a religion of resentment or a religion for idiots, but because God can be known only when one freely accepts to be embraced by the will of the Son. The man whose only desire is to be an adult makes himself a god and thereby loses both God and his own self. But where he continues to say "Father", he realizes what sonship and knowledge and freedom mean. All these mean belonging to God, and that is our salvation.

"Piscatorie, non Aristotelice": since the Fathers of Nicaea were not ashamed to belong to the crowd of the immature, they were allowed to take part in the praise of the Father. In this praise, the will of the Son is disclosed and becomes the redemption of those who labor and are heavy laden. Let us ask the Son to grant that we, too, may dwell in the sphere of his will, that we may become sons through him, the consubstantial Son, and thereby receive the freedom of salvation.

# Risen from the dead in accordance with Scripture[18]

The dispute about the Resurrection of Jesus from the dead has broken out with new vehemence and has penetrated the very heart of the Church today. The debate is fueled not only by the general crisis affecting traditional values, but also specifically by the form taken by the tradition that tells us about the Resurrection. The fact that the biblical texts must be translated from the world of the past into the world of the present not only linguistically, but also in terms of their ideas, makes it seem obvious that in this instance, too, an act of translation might be required that would overturn many of the ideas to which we are accustomed. This impression is reinforced when one compares the individual Resurrection narratives with each other, for their differences are obvious, and we can see that they stammer in their attempt to translate into words an event for which our customary language clearly has no sufficient means of expression. The question of how to distinguish the kernel from the husk here cannot be avoided, and it is difficult to decide what is falsification and what is a genuine translation.

I shall not attempt in this meditation to discuss the various contemporary theories about this; all I shall do is to

---

[18] Recent German scholarship is presented by L. Scheffczyk, *Auferstehung: Prinzip christlichen Glaubens* (Einsiedeln, 1976); on the exegetical discussion, cf. especially B. Rigaux, *Dieu l'a ressuscité* (Gembloux: Duculot, 1973).

set out as positively as possible the recognizable center of the biblical testimony. One who reads the New Testament will have no great difficulty in grasping that there are two essentially different types of tradition concerning the Resurrection. One of these might be called the "confessional tradition", the other the "narrative tradition". The first type is exemplified in verses 3–8 of the fifteenth chapter of 1 Corinthians; the second type is found in the Resurrection narratives of the four Gospels. The two types arose in different ways with very different questions underlying them; each has different intentions and tasks. Accordingly, the kind of claim each type makes is different, and this is very significant for the task of exposition and for the identification of the core of the message.

We can glimpse the origin of the confessional tradition in the narrative tradition, which relates that the Emmaus disciples return to Jerusalem and are greeted by the Eleven with the cry: "The Lord has risen indeed, and has appeared to Simon!" (Lk 24:34). This sentence may be the oldest surviving text about the Resurrection.[19] At any rate, the formation of the tradition begins with such simple acclamations, which gradually become an invariable element in the assemblies of the disciples and take on a fixed formulation. They are now a confession of faith in the presence of the Lord, an expression of hope, and at the same time the distinguishing mark that allows the believers to recognize each other. The Christian profession of faith emerges. The creed that Paul explicitly preserves as a tradition in 1 Corinthians 15:3–8 was elaborated at a very early point in this process of tradition, probably in Palestine as early as the thirties. It was entrusted to him for safekeeping, and

---

[19] On this, cf. H. Schlier, *Über die Auferstehung Jesu Christi* (Einsiedeln, 1968), especially p. 7; J. Jeremias, *Neutestamentliche Theologie* I (1971), p. 291.

he hands it on in the same manner. These very ancient creedal texts are concerned only on a secondary level with supplying what we today would call "information about the faith"; as Paul emphasizes, their real purpose is to hold fast the Christian kernel, for without this, both the message and the faith would be nothing.

The narrative tradition grew from another impulse: people wanted to know what happened. There was an increasing demand to get close to the events and to have detailed information. Very early on, Christians also found it necessary to defend themselves against suspicions, against all the various attacks that we can sense when we read the Gospel, as well as against the false interpretations that were already beginning in Corinth. These factors demanded substantial narratives in greater detail, and such needs then led to the formation of the more circumstantial tradition of the Gospels. Accordingly, each of the two traditions is indispensable in its own way; but at the same time, we can see that there is a hierarchy. The confessional tradition is superior to the narrative tradition. The confessional tradition is really "the faith" that provides the criteria for every interpretation.

Accordingly, let us try to understand somewhat more exactly the fundamental creed that Paul has preserved. This must be the starting point of every attempt to arrive at decisions in the clash of opinions. Paul (or, rather, his creed) begins with the death of Jesus, and it is striking that this bare text, which says not one word too many, adds two phrases to the information "he died": first, "in accordance with the Scriptures", and secondly, "for our sins". What does this mean?

The affirmation "in accordance with the Scriptures" locates the event in the context of the Old Testament history of God's covenant with his people. This death is not a chance occurrence unconnected to anything else; rather, it belongs in the context of *this* divine history, which gives it its logic and its significance. It is an event in which words of Scripture are fulfilled, that is, an event with an inherent *logos*, logic, an event that proceeds from the Word and enters into the Word, guaranteeing its truth and fulfilling it. The event proceeds from the history of God's Word among men. The second phrase tells us how this verbal character is to be understood: it was a dying "for our sins". This creedal formula takes up a prophetic text (Is 53:12; cf. also 53:7–11). In other words, its reference to "the Scriptures" is not some vague allusion. It intones an Old Testament melody with which the believers were familiar, thanks to the collections of biblical "testimonies to Christ" that were made at an early date.[20] This takes the death of Jesus out of the trajectory of the death that was laden with a curse, a death that began at the tree of knowledge, with man's presumptuous desire to become God's equal. At the end of this trajectory, man, far from being a god, is merely earth. Jesus' death is of a different kind. It is not the carrying out of a verdict that casts man back into the earth; rather, it is the action of a love that will not leave the others bereft of word, bereft of meaning, bereft of eternity. Jesus' death is to be understood, not in the context of the judicial sentence that expelled man from paradise, but rather in the light of the Songs of the Suffering Servant. Since his death takes place in the spirit of these words, it becomes a light for the peoples, a death in the context of his service of expiation, which desires to bring about reconciliation. And this means that his death

---

[20] On the early Christian collections of testimonies, cf. J. Daniélou, "Das Leben, das am Holze hängt", in *Kirche und Überlieferung*, ed. J. Betz and H. Fries, pp. 22–34 (Freiburg, 1960).

puts an end to death. Thus, when we look in detail at
the text, we see that the double interpretation that our
creedal text adds after the words "Christ died" opens up
the path from the Cross to the Resurrection. For what is
affirmed here is far more than an interpretation: it is an
inner dimension of the event itself.

The scriptural passage goes on to state, harshly and without any commentary: "He was buried." This can be understood only in the light of what precedes and what follows.
First of all, it states that Jesus genuinely experienced death
to the full. He was laid in the pit of death. He descended
into the world of the dead, into the underworld. The
Church's faith later reflected very vividly on this mystery of
Jesus' experience of death and took precisely this as its starting point in its attempt to grasp how his victory encompassed all of history and the world.[21] A different question
confronts us very urgently today: Does the tomb play any
role for faith? Does it have anything to do with the Resurrection of the Lord? This is where the clash of opinions
begins today. The debate concerns the kind of realism that
is required by the Christian message. The arguments seem
very plausible: What is this miracle of a resuscitated corpse
supposed to mean? What could the point be? Is this conflict
with the laws of nature worthy of the Word of God? Does
it not prevent us from seeing something that could in fact
be relevant to us here and now?

As soon as we hear these questions, immensely important counterquestions arise. When the event of the Resurrection is transformed into the recognition of a mission, of

---

[21] On the question of Jesus' descent into Hades, cf. especially Hans Urs von
Balthasar, *Theologie der drei Tage* (Einsiedeln, 1969), and *Spirit and Institution*,
trans. Edward T. Oakes, S.J., Explorations in Theology 4 (San Francisco: Ignatius Press, 1995), pp. 401–14.

a continuing task, or of an abiding significance of Jesus, is this not merely an escape, something that robs faith in the Resurrection of its reality? Does not the contemptuous dismissal of what is called the miracle of a resuscitated corpse actually display a contempt for the body that is both unchristian and anthropologically false? Is there not a secret skepticism behind this that deprives God of the possibility of acting in the world? What is in fact being promised, when it is clear that nothing is promised to the human body?

We must of course admit that our creedal text does not speak of the empty tomb. Its immediate interest lies, not in the emptiness of the tomb, but in the fact that Jesus had lain in it. We must also admit that if one were to understand the Resurrection on the basis of the tomb alone— that is, resurrection as the antithesis of burial—this would not do justice to the New Testament message, since Jesus is not one who returned from the dead like the young man at Nain and Lazarus, who were summoned back into an earthly life that subsequently ended with their definitive deaths. The Resurrection of Jesus is not like the reversal of clinical death that we know about today, for this, too, ends at some later date with a clinical death that can no longer be reversed. The difference is made clear not only by the evangelists, but also by our creedal text itself, which goes on to describe the appearances of the risen Jesus with the Greek word ὤφθη. This is usually translated as "he appeared", but it would be more correct to say: "He allowed himself to be seen." This formula shows that something different is involved here, that Jesus after the Resurrection belongs to a sphere of reality that is normally inaccessible to our senses. Only this can explain a point on which all the evangelists agree, namely, that Jesus was unrecognizable. He no longer belongs to the world that is perceptible to our senses: he now belongs to the world of God, and hence one can see him only if he allows himself to be seen. And *this* act of seeing makes demands of the heart, the spirit, and the inner openness of a man. Even in our normal daily living, the act of seeing is not as banal as we usually suppose. Two people who look at the world simultaneously seldom see exactly the same, since we always see from within. This means that one can perceive the beauty of things or only their usefulness. In the face of another, one can note the anxiety, the love, the concealed distress, the hidden untruthfulness, but one can also fail to see any of this. Although all this appears to the senses, it is *perceived* only in a process that involves both the senses and the mind. And this process makes greater demands on us when the revelation of something to our senses reaches deeper into the foundation of reality. Something similar is true of the risen Lord: he shows himself to the senses, yet he can only make use of senses that see beyond what can be perceived by the senses.

Accordingly, the text as a whole obliges us to say that the risen Jesus certainly did not live in the manner of one resuscitated from the dead. He lived out of the very heart of the divine power, above the zone of that which is physically and chemically measurable. At the same time, however, it was truly he himself, this person, the Jesus who had been executed two days earlier, who lived. And our text states this very explicitly in its sequence of two separate affirmations. First, we read: "He was raised on the third day in accordance with the Scriptures", and then we read: "He appeared to Cephas, then to the Twelve." The Resurrection and the appearing are clearly separate, independent elements in the profession of faith. The Resurrection is more than the appearances; and the appearances are not the Resurrection but are only its radiant splendor. First, the Resurrection is an *event* that happens to Jesus himself, between the Father and him in the power of the Holy Spirit; then, this event that happens to Jesus himself becomes *accessible* to men, because he makes it accessible.

This brings us back to the question about the tomb, which we can now answer. The tomb is not the center of the Resurrection message; the center is the Lord in his new life. Nevertheless, the tomb cannot be eliminated from this message. When this extremely concentrated text mentions the burial of Jesus so succinctly, it clearly intends to say that this burial was not the last step of Jesus' earthly path. The words that immediately follow, speaking of the Resurrection "on the third day", are an implicit allusion to Psalm 16 [15]:10, which is one of the principal elements of the apostolic "proof from the Scriptures". As we see in the early Christian sermons that have been transmitted to us by the Acts of the Apostles, this text must be considered the primary reference of the phrase "according to the Scriptures". This verse states: "You do not give me up to Sheol, or let your godly one see the Pit" of corruption. The Jews held that corruption began after the third day; the words of Scripture are fulfilled in Jesus by his Resurrection on the third day, before corruption set in. The words about Jesus' burial go together with the preceding words about his death: all this takes place within the framework of Scripture. The new death that Jesus dies leads to the tomb, but not to corruption. It is the death of death. This death is held fast in the Word of God and thus belongs to the life that snatches away death's power at the point where it destroys the physical body and dissolves man into the earth.[22]

---

[22] Cf. J. Kremer, *Das älteste Zeugnis von der Auferstehung Christi* (Stuttgart, 1966), pp. 37–54; on "the third day", cf. especially K. Lehmann, *Auferweckt am dritten Tag nach der Schrift* (Freiburg, 1968); J. Blank, *Paulus und Jesus* (Munich, 1968), pp. 153–56, in the context of his discussion of Paul's belief in the Resurrection (pp. 133–83).

This conquering of the power of death at the exact place where it becomes irrevocable is a central element in the biblical testimony—quite apart from the fact that it would have been completely impossible to proclaim the Resurrection of Jesus if everyone could know and ascertain that he still lay in the tomb. That would be impossible even in our own society, where theoretical experiments are conducted with concepts of "resurrection" for which the body is irrelevant; and it would have been all the more impossible in the Jewish world, where a man was his body, not something apart from it. One who professes his faith in this is not claiming that a weird miracle took place. He is affirming the power of God, who respects his creation but is not bound by its laws governing death. It is of course true that death is the fundamental shape of the world that exists today; but the conquering of death, its abolition in reality and not merely in thought, is something that man desires and seeks today just as much as in the past. The Resurrection of Jesus says that this conquering is in fact possible. Death does not belong fundamentally and irrevocably to the structure of creation, to matter. Naturally, the Resurrection also says that the boundary posed by death will not be overcome by more refined clinical techniques and technology. This is done by the creative power of the Word and of love. Only these powers are strong enough to change the structure of matter so fundamentally that it becomes possible to overcome the barrier of death. This means that the extraordinary promise of this event also contains an extraordinary appeal, a mission, a whole interpretation of human existence and of the world.

Above all, however, we can see that faith in the Resurrection of Jesus is a profession of faith in the real existence of God and in his creation, in God's unconditional affirmation of creation and of matter. The Word of God genuinely penetrates the body. His power does not come to a halt at the border of matter. It embraces everything. And this is why the responsibility to which this Word summons us also penetrates matter and the body and proves itself there. Ultimately, faith in the Resurrection concerns the genuine power of God and the extent of human responsibility. God's power means hope and joy: this is the redeeming essence of its revelation at Easter, which allows us to sing Alleluia in the midst of a world that lies under the heavy shadow of death.

# 3

# The Holy Spirit

We believe in God the Father, the Son, and the Holy Spirit, the triune God. But while we are able to say rather a lot about the Father and the Son, the Holy Spirit has largely remained the unknown God. In the course of Church history, there have always been those who appealed to the Holy Spirit, but the result of the movements that arose in this way was often that the Church spoke even *less* about the Holy Spirit.

This begins with Mani (216–274 or 277),[1] the father of Manichaeism, who claimed to be the incarnation of the Paraclete—the Holy Spirit—and therefore superior to Christ. A dark shadow spreads from there through the entire Church history of the Middle Ages: the arrogant claim to a higher holiness, which, despite all attempts at resistance, darkened the faith of Christendom. It was hard for the Church to throw off this inheritance. Nourished by other roots, the "Spirit" movement of Montanism found many adherents in the Church in Asia Minor in the second century. Its most eloquent Western representative was the great ecclesiastical writer Tertullian (ca. 160–after 220). The Montanist message led him to despise the "sinful Church", an attitude that ended in arrogance and a gloomy moralism.

The most fascinating form of the yearning for the Holy Spirit was formulated by a pious abbot in southern Italy in the twelfth century, Joachim of Fiore (ca. 1130–1202). Joachim was deeply conscious of the deficiencies of the Church in his time: the hatred that separated Jews and Christians, the old and the new people of God, from one

[1] On Mani and Manichaeism, cf. A. Adam, *Lehrbuch der Dogmengeschichte* 1 (Gütersloh, 1965), pp. 207–10; H.-C. Puech, in *Lexikon für Theologie und Kirche*, 2nd ed., 6, cols. 1351–55.

another; the hostility between the Church of the East and the Church of the West; the jealousy between clergy and laity; the high-handedness and greed for power displayed by the Church's men. This led him to the conviction that this could not yet be the definitive form of the Church of God on earth and that before the return of Christ at the end of the world, God must take a new step on *this* earth, in this history. He longed for a Church that would be truly in accordance with the New Testament and the promises of the prophets and, indeed, with the deepest yearnings of man's heart, a Church in which Jews and Gentiles, East and West, clergy and laity would live in the spirit of truth and of love, without precepts and laws, so that the will of God for his creature man would be genuinely fulfilled. Out of this grew his new vision, in which he attempted to interpret the rhythm of history on the basis of the trinitarian image of God. After the kingdom of the Father in the Old Testament and the kingdom of the Son in the hierarchical Church that had existed up to then, a third kingdom, a kingdom of the Holy Spirit, would come from around 1260 onward. This would be a kingdom of freedom and of universal peace.

For Joachim, such ideas were more than mere speculations about the future, a consolation in view of the inadequacy of the present day. In his eyes, they had a very practical character, since he believed he had discovered that the individual periods did not follow in a cleanly separated sequence. He saw overlappings, in which the dawning of the new already penetrated the old. He saw the New Covenant dawning in the midst of the Old Covenant, in the faith and piety of the prophets; and in the monks' form of life, the coming Church already penetrated the Church of the present. This meant that one had to go to meet the future, one had to take up one's position in the movement of history, as it were, on the escalator that leads into the future.

He himself attempted to do so by founding a new monastic community that would lead the way and open the door into the new age. This also shows how he envisaged the future. The "eternal gospel" of which he spoke (with an allusion to Revelation 14:6) was ultimately nothing other than the gospel of Jesus Christ. Accordingly, the working of the Holy Spirit and of his gospel would mean that now at last the first gospel, the Sermon on the Mount, would be observed fully. The gospel, taken literally, would be the wholly spiritual Christianity—this is his vision.

Since then, the hope that Joachim expressed by appealing to the definitive coming of the Holy Spirit has never left men in peace. First came the Franciscans, who saw the new Church beginning in their movement. In the struggles that this claim unleashed between the various wings of the order, however, the hope lost its spiritual luster. It became harsher and more combative, and now those who spread this hope in Italy were groups who sought a political renewal. We need not follow the details of the subsequent history of this idea here; but it is noteworthy that the slogans "Third Reich" and "Führer/Duce" of Hitler and Mussolini go back by various routes to Joachim's heritage. Via Hegel, Marxism, too, adopted something of his vision: the idea of a history that marches forward in triumph, infallibly reaching its goal, and hence the idea of the definitive realization of salvation within history.[2]

---

[2] On Joachim of Fiore and the history of his influence, cf. especially E. Benz, *Ecclesia spiritualis: Kirchenidee und Geschichtstheologie der franziskanischen Reformation* (Stuttgart, 1934); K. Löwith, *Weltgeschichte und Heilsgeschehen* (Stuttgart, 1953), pp. 136–47; A. Dempf, *Sacrum Imperium* (1929; Darmstadt, 1954), especially pp. 269–84. On the reception and transformation of Joachim's ideas in Franciscan theology, cf. also Joseph Ratzinger, *The Theology of History in St. Bonaventure*, trans. Zachary Hayes, O.F.M. (Chicago: Franciscan Herald Press, 1989). On the theology of history outlined by Saint Irenaeus, which has the opposite structure, cf. the dissertation by R. Tremblay, *La Manifestation et la vision de Dieu selon St. Irénée de Lyon*, Münsterer Theologische Studien 41 (Münster, 1978).

It is worth speaking in such detail about Joachim because he makes particularly clear both the potential and the risks of speaking about the Holy Spirit. There is something path-breaking in Joachim's willingness to begin here and now with a truly "spiritual" Christianity and to see this spiritual Christianity, not beyond the Word, but in the innermost depths of the Word itself. There was thus some truth in the early Franciscans' view of Joachim's doctrine as a prophetic premonition of the figure of Saint Francis, for Francis gave the most beautiful answer to Joachim. Indeed, this was the only correct response, for Francis' life was a winnowing fork that separated the spiritual and the demonic in Joachim's work (something that the saint's successors could not do). His motto was: "sine glossa" (without a commentary). He sought to live Sacred Scripture, and especially the Sermon on the Mount, without making fine distinctions and without evasions. He wanted the Word to take him at his word. Something that is distorted by all kinds of speculations in Joachim became perfectly unambiguous in Francis, and this is why he has been such a radiant figure down through the centuries: the Christianity of the Spirit is the Christianity of the lived Word. The Spirit dwells in the Word, not in a departure from the Word. The Word is the location of the Spirit; Jesus is the source of the Spirit. The more we enter into him, the more really do we enter into the Spirit, and the Spirit enters into us. This also exposes the false element in Joachim, namely, the utopia of a Church that would depart from the Son and rise higher than him and the irrational expectation that portrays itself as a real and rational program.

This gives us an initial outline of a theology of the Holy Spirit. I have said that we come to see the Spirit, not by departing from the Son, but by entering into him. In his account of the first appearance of the risen Jesus to the

Eleven, John captures this truth in an eloquent image: the Spirit is the breath of the Son. One receives him by coming within breathing range of the Son, by letting the Son breathe into one (Jn 20:19–23). This is why Irenaeus' sketch of the trinitarian logic of history is much more correct than Joachim's. For Irenaeus, this is not an ascent from the Father to the Son and then finally to liberation, to the Spirit. Within history, the direction taken by the Persons is the exact opposite of this: the Spirit is present at the beginning as an instruction and guidance of man that is as yet scarcely perceptible. He leads to the Son and, through the Son, to the Father ...

This insight agrees with what the Fathers attempt to say about the Being of the Holy Spirit. Unlike "Father" and "Son", the name of the third Divine Person is not the expression of something specific. It designates that which is common in the Godhead. But this reveals the "proper character" of the third Person: he is that which is common, the unity of the Father and the Son, the unity in Person. The Father and the Son are one with each other by going out beyond themselves; it is in the third Person, in the fruitfulness of their act of giving, that they are One.

It is of course true that such affirmations are never more than faltering glimpses. We can never know the Spirit otherwise than in what he accomplishes. This is why Scripture never describes the Spirit in himself. It tells us only how he comes to man and how he can be distinguished from other spirits.

Let us look at some of these texts. In the Gospel that used to be read at Pentecost (Jn 14:22–31), Jude Thaddeus asks the Lord a question that has occurred to us all in some fashion. He has understood Jesus' words to mean that he wishes to show himself only to his disciples, and so he says: "Lord, how is it that you will manifest yourself to us, and not to the world?" Jesus' reply seems to avoid this question: "If a man loves me, he will keep my word, and my Father will love him, and we will come to him and make our home with him." But in reality, this is precisely the reply to the disciple's question (and our own) about the Spirit. One cannot display the Spirit of God as one displays goods for sale in a shop. He can be seen only by the one who bears him within himself. Seeing and coming, seeing and dwelling belong inseparably together here. The Holy Spirit dwells in Jesus' Word, and one possesses this Word, not through mere talking, but by keeping it, by living it. He who is the life of the Word lives in the lived Word.

The ancient Church reflected on this above all in connection with Psalm 68 [67], which was read as a hymn about the Ascension of Christ and the sending of the Holy Spirit. When the Old Testament is read in this manner, the Church understands the ascent of Moses as an image of the Pentecost event. Moses ascended not only externally, but also internally. He exposed himself to solitude with God. Because he survived the heights, the cloud, and the solitary dialogue with God, he was able to bring men the Spirit in the form of a word that gave guidance. The Spirit is the fruit of his ascent and of his solitary experiences. Considered from the perspective of the New Testament, both this path taken by Moses and the gift that he makes in the Spirit—the word of the law—are only a shadow and a preliminary manifestation of what took place in Jesus. It was he who truly took human nature, our flesh, into the dialogue with God when he was borne through the cloud of death to see the face of God. Out of this ascent came the Spirit, who is the fruit of Jesus' victory, the fruit of his love—the fruit of the Cross.

With this in mind, we can attempt to say something that gives at least some notion of the inner mystery of God.

The Father and the Son are the movement of pure mutual giving, pure mutual handing over of oneself. In this movement, they are fruitful, and their fruitfulness is their unity, their complete oneness, but it is a unity in which they themselves are neither canceled out nor dissolved into each other. For us men, giving and yielding ourselves up always means the cross. In the world, the trinitarian mystery is translated into a mystery of the cross: it is there that we find the fruitfulness out of which the Holy Spirit comes.

John strongly emphasizes that the Spirit dwells, not alongside the Word, but in it, when he says that the Spirit's activity in history consists in recalling. Jesus tells us that the Holy Spirit speaks, not out of what is his own, but "out of what is mine". He can be recognized by his fidelity to the Word that was once uttered in the past. Here, John constructs a strict parallel between Christology and pneumatology, for Christ, too, reveals what he is when he says: "My teaching is not mine" (7:16). This selflessness, this lack of autonomy, is his real authentication before the world; but the Antichrist can be recognized precisely by the fact that he speaks in his own name. The same is true of the Holy Spirit. He shows that he is the trinitarian Spirit, the Spirit of the one God in three Persons, precisely by not appearing as a separate and separable self, but by disappearing into the Son and into the Father. The impossibility of elaborating a separate pneumatology belongs to the essence of the Spirit.

In the context of the doctrinal struggles of his own age, John very consciously formulated these affirmations as a litmus test to distinguish between the Spirit of God and the evil spirit. The great leaders of gnosis became interesting precisely by speaking in their own name—they made a name for themselves. They were exciting because they had something new to say, something that went beyond the Word: for example, that Jesus in reality did not die but danced with his disciples while people thought he was hanging on the Cross. The fourth Gospel consciously counters such gnostic novelties, such acts of speaking in one's own name, by employing the ecclesial plural: the one who speaks disappears into the "we" of the Church, which truly gives a man his own proper countenance and saves him from crumbling away into nothingness. The same pattern is followed in the Letters of John, where the author is simply called "the elder"; his adversary is the *pro-agōn*, "the one who goes ahead" (2 Jn 9). Like the Letters, the Gospel of John in its entirety seeks to be nothing other than an act of remembering. And this is what makes it the Gospel of the Spirit. It is fruitful, new, and deep precisely in virtue of the fact that it does not think up new systems; rather, it remembers. The Being of the Holy Spirit, as the unity of Father and Son, is the selflessness of remembering, and this selflessness is the true renewal. The Church of the Spirit is the Church that recalls and understands more deeply, penetrates farther into the Word, and thus becomes richer and more alive. True selflessness, pointing away from oneself into the totality, is thus the mark of the Spirit, the image of his trinitarian Being.

Let us look briefly at the Pauline writings. Paul is confronted in the Corinthian community by an almost child-like joy in the gifts of the Spirit that is beginning to pose a threat to the essential reality. People want to outdo each other; their attention is more and more directed to outward appearances and external things, and they are gradually turning into a sect. Paul counters this with the insight that only *one* gift is important, namely, love (1 Cor 13). Without it, everything else is nothing. And love reveals itself in unity; it is the opposite of sectarianism. It reveals itself in building up and in supporting. It is the Holy Spirit who builds up. But where things are torn down and bitterness, envy, and hostility grow, the Holy Spirit is not present. Knowledge without love is not from him. Here, the Pauline and the Johannine thinking concur, since John would say that love reveals itself in "abiding". Ultimately, this is exactly what is affirmed by Paul's doctrine of the body of Christ.[3]

Paul and John agree essentially on yet another point. John calls the Spirit "Paraclete", that is, advocate, helper, defender, comforter. He is thus the adversary of the *diabolos*, the "prosecutor", the slanderer, "who accuses [our brethren] day and night before our God" (Rev 12:10). The Spirit is the Yes, just as Christ is the Yes. Correspondingly, Paul emphasizes joy very strongly. We may say that the Spirit is the Spirit of joy and of the Gospel. One of the basic rules for the discernment of spirits could be formulated as follows: Where joylessness rules and humor dies, we may be certain that the Holy Spirit, the Spirit of Jesus Christ, is not present. Furthermore, joy is a sign of grace. One who is serene from the bottom of his heart, one who has suffered without losing joy, is not far from the God of the Gospel, from the Spirit of God, who is the Spirit of eternal joy.

---

[3] On this, cf. my essay: "Der Heilige Geist als communio: Zum Verhältnis von Pneumatologie und Spiritualität bei Augustinus", in *Erfahrung und Theologie des Heiligen Geistes*, ed. C. Heitmann and H. Mühlen, pp. 223–38 (Hamburg and Munich, 1974); I recommend this volume as a whole, in which many authors speak about the Holy Spirit. A very important work on pneumatology is likewise M.J. Le Guillou, *Les Témoins sont parmi nous: L'Expérience de Dieu dans l'Esprit Saint* (Paris, 1976).